READINGS ON

THE IMPORTANCE OF BEING EARNEST

READINGS ON

THE IMPORTANCE
OF BEING EARNEST

OTHER TITLES IN THE GREENHAVEN PRESS LITERARY COMPANION SERIES:

BRITISH AUTHORS

Jane Austen
Joseph Conrad
Charles Dickens
J.R.R. Tolkien

BRITISH LITERATURE

Animal Farm
Beowulf
Brave New World
The Canterbury Tales
A Christmas Carol
Frankenstein
Great Expectations
Gulliver's Travels
Hamlet
Heart of Darkness
Jane Eyre
Julius Caesar
Lord of the Flies

Macbeth
The Merchant of Venice
A Midsummer Night's
 Dream
Oliver Twist
Othello
A Portrait of the Artist
 as a Young Man
Pride and Prejudice
Romeo and Juliet
Shakespeare: The Comedies
Shakespeare: The Histories
Shakespeare: The Sonnets
Shakespeare: The Tragedies
Silas Marner
A Tale of Two Cities
The Taming of the Shrew
Tess of the d'Urbervilles
Twelfth Night
Wuthering Heights

THE GREENHAVEN PRESS
Literary Companion
TO BRITISH LITERATURE

READINGS ON

THE IMPORTANCE OF BEING EARNEST

Thomas Siebold, *Book Editor*

Bonnie Szumski, *Series Editor*

Greenhaven Press, Inc., San Diego, CA

Library of Congress Cataloging-in-Publication Data

Readings on The importance of being earnest /
   Thomas Siebold, book editor.
       p. cm. — (Greenhaven Press literary companion to British literature)
   Includes bibliographical references and index.
   ISBN 0-7377-0560-4 (alk. paper) —
ISBN 0-7377-0559-0 (pbk. : alk. paper)
   1. Wilde, Oscar, 1854–1900. Importance of being earnest. I. Title: Importance of being earnest. II. Siebold, Thomas. III. Series.

PR5818.I45 R43 2001
822'.8—dc21
                                                    00-059323
                                                    CIP

Copyright © 2001 by Greenhaven Press, Inc.
PO Box 289009
San Diego, CA 92198-9009
Printed in the U.S.A.

"The truth is rarely pure and never simple."

—Oscar Wilde, *The Importance of Being Earnest*

CONTENTS

Foreword   11

Introduction   13

Oscar Wilde: A Biography   15

Characters and Plot   35

Chapter 1: Wilde's Use of Language in *The Importance of Being Earnest*

1. **The Importance of Being Earnest as a**
   Verbal Opera *by Alan Bird*   44
   The Importance of Being Earnest is like a verbal opera:
   Wilde uses clever dialogue like operatic arias, relegating
   some dramatic elements to secondary status. Also like
   opera, the plot hinges on secrets and schemes.

2. **The Play's World of Linguistic Pleasure**
   by Julia Prewitt Brown   51
   The characters in the play are beyond the determinism of
   the past; they wander in a linguistic world where no one
   sacrifices or suffers. Whereas the characters in Victorian
   novels often learn to bear suffering, the characters in
   Wilde's play learn to "bear" pleasure.

3. **Wilde as a Master Epigrammist** *by Francesca Coppa*   57
   Oscar Wilde is a master epigrammist and *The Importance
   of Being Earnest* is an epigrammatic play. Wilde cites and
   reworks established knowledge, allowing audience members to share his position of authority.

4. **Wilde's Painstaking Writing Process**
   by Russell Jackson   65
   Wilde was a careful craftsman who revised his work meticulously. *The Importance of Being Earnest* omits many of the
   stock characters and the overall decadent tone that distinguished his earlier work.

5. **Bunbury Sources** *by William Green*   74
   Wilde was fascinated with names, often using place names,
   attributive names, or names of people whom he knew in

his work. "Bunbury" refers to two actual individuals known to Wilde.

6. The Language of the Dandy
by Patricia Flanagan Behrendt 83
In *The Importance of Being Earnest* Wilde adroitly renders the language of the dandy, which is both penetratingly humorous and highly aggressive. It is language that manipulates viewers into laughing at topics and situations that they would not normally find inherently funny.

Chapter 2: Characterization in *The Importance of Being Earnest*

1. Duplicity in *The Importance of Being Earnest*
by Joseph Bristow 91
In *The Importance of Being Earnest* things are never what they seem: Characters have double lives, the city and the country represent two different sets of values, and the ritual of eating contrasts the propriety of high society and sexual desire.

2. Speranza: The Mother Figure in *The Importance of Being Earnest* by Patrick M. Horan
97
Wilde's portrayal of a mother figure in the play captures the dualistic nature of his own mother, Speranza. Lady Bracknell represents Speranza's conventional side while Miss Prism represents her artistic side.

3. Marriage and Women *by Sos Eltis*
105
In his extensive revision of *The Importance of Being Earnest*, Oscar Wilde made Gwendolen and Cecily more confident, stylish, and determined. Moreover, in the final version of the play the sexes are equally balanced and marriage is viewed with much less cynicism.

4. *The Importance of Being Earnest* and Social Masks *by Norbert Kohl*
114
The comedy in *The Importance of Being Earnest* stems from the unexpected contrast between the seriousness of situations and the trivial, superficial responses of the characters to those situations. Throughout the play the characters replace an anticipated emotional involvement with severe intellectual detachment.

Chapter 3: Philosophy, Themes, and Meaning in *The Importance of Being Earnest*

1. Wilde's Attack on Seriousness *by Philip K. Cohen* 125
In *The Importance of Being Earnest* Wilde creates a fairy tale atmosphere in which harsh realities are transformed by

laughter and even suffering and death are robbed of their power.

2. *The Importance of Being Earnest* as an
   Anglo-Irish Parable *by Declan Kiberd*   132
   The role of the double in *The Importance of Being Earnest*
   reflects the strained, symbiotic relations between England
   and Ireland.

3. **The Philosophy of the Dandy** *by Arthur Ganz*   140
   Wilde embraces an attitude toward life called dandyism.
   The dandy is a self-absorbed, intense individualist who rejects both the content and moral standards of middle-class
   society.

4. **Wilde's Vision of Nothingness** *by David Parker*   152
   In his farce, Wilde contemplates a vision of nothingness in
   which identity and the structures, values, and morals of society melt into insubstantiality. Truth, like identity, becomes
   an individual act of imagination built on a proliferation of
   deceptive and contradictory impressions.

Chapter 4: Genre and Structure in *The Importance of Being Earnest*

1. **Wilde's Use of Ironic Counterpoint**
   by Eric Bentley   161
   Wilde takes potshots at the problems of society but never
   really crosses into satire or harsh criticism. Throughout the
   play Wilde maintains an ironic counterpoint between the
   outward elegance and assuredness of the characters and
   their inner emptiness.

2. **The Tedium of *The Importance of Being Earnest***
   by Mary McCarthy   167
   Wilde imposes his opinions on the audience and his outrageous characters become monotonous. Repeated jokes,
   stock characters, and paradoxical humor become tedious.

3. ***The Importance of Being Earnest* as Self-Parody**
   by Christopher S. Nassaar   171
   In *The Importance of Being Earnest* Wilde parodies his earlier works, reducing their intellectual content to harmless
   absurdity.

Chronology   178

For Further Research   180

Index   182

FOREWORD

*"'Tis the good reader that
makes the good book."*

Ralph Waldo Emerson

The story's bare facts are simple: The captain, an old and scarred seafarer, walks with a peg leg made of whale ivory. He relentlessly drives his crew to hunt the world's oceans for the great white whale that crippled him. After a long search, the ship encounters the whale and a fierce battle ensues. Finally the captain drives his harpoon into the whale, but the harpoon line catches the captain about the neck and drags him to his death.

A simple story, a straightforward plot—yet, since the 1851 publication of Herman Melville's *Moby-Dick*, readers and critics have found many meanings in the struggle between Captain Ahab and the whale. To some, the novel is a cautionary tale that depicts how Ahab's obsession with revenge leads to his insanity and death. Others believe that the whale represents the unknowable secrets of the universe and that Ahab is a tragic hero who dares to challenge fate by attempting to discover this knowledge. Perhaps Melville intended Ahab as a criticism of Americans' tendency to become involved in well-intentioned but irrational causes. Or did Melville model Ahab after himself, letting his fictional character express his anger at what he perceived as a cruel and distant god?

Although literary critics disagree over the meaning of *Moby-Dick*, readers do not need to choose one particular interpretation in order to gain an understanding of Melville's novel. Instead, by examining various analyses, they can gain numerous insights into the issues that lie under the surface of the basic plot. Studying the writings of literary critics can also aid readers in making their own assessments of *Moby-Dick* and other literary works and in developing analytical thinking skills.

The Greenhaven Literary Companion Series was created with these goals in mind. Designed for young adults, this unique anthology series provides an engaging and comprehensive introduction to literary analysis and criticism. The essays included in the Literary Companion Series are chosen for their accessibility to a young adult audience and are expertly edited in consideration of both the reading and comprehension levels of this audience. In addition, each essay is introduced by a concise summation that presents the contributing writer's main themes and insights. Every anthology in the Literary Companion Series contains a varied selection of critical essays that cover a wide time span and express diverse views. Wherever possible, primary sources are represented through excerpts from authors' notebooks, letters, and journals and through contemporary criticism.

Each title in the Literary Companion Series pays careful consideration to the historical context of the particular author or literary work. In-depth biographies and detailed chronologies reveal important aspects of authors' lives and emphasize the historical events and social milieu that influenced their writings. To facilitate further research, every anthology includes primary and secondary source bibliographies of articles and/or books selected for their suitability for young adults. These engaging features make the Greenhaven Literary Companion series ideal for introducing students to literary analysis in the classroom or as a library resource for young adults researching the world's great authors and literature.

Exceptional in its focus on young adults, the Greenhaven Literary Companion Series strives to present literary criticism in a compelling and accessible format. Every title in the series is intended to spark readers' interest in leading American and world authors, to help them broaden their understanding of literature, and to encourage them to formulate their own analyses of the literary works that they read. It is the editors' hope that young adult readers will find these anthologies to be true companions in their study of literature.

INTRODUCTION

The audiences that first saw Oscar Wilde's *The Importance of Being Earnest* in 1895 loved it, but the critics were somewhat baffled. Of course the critics were amused, but when it came time to write their reviews, they did not know how to respond to the play. Some reviewers criticized its lack of characterization and its absurdity of plot; others, like the noted playwright and critic George Bernard Shaw, complained that the laughter was empty because the play lacked depth and substance. Despite some of the mixed and rather cool critical responses to the play, the theater was packed every night. Unfortunately, shortly after its opening Oscar Wilde became embroiled in a highly publicized sex scandal and attendance dropped precipitously, forcing management to close the play early. Wilde suffered a devastating disgrace, and his career was essentially over. After his death in 1900 Wilde's reputation as a playwright regained momentum with revival performances of *The Importance of Being Earnest*, and today critics and playgoers consider it to be one of the funniest plays written in English.

The play centers on two couples who have fallen in love and want to marry. Before the lovers can reach their goal, however, they must transverse through a Wildean world of inversions, ambiguities, absurdity, social masks, double identities, digressions, and irreverence. Wilde admitted that while writing the play he "was struck by madness from the moon." Because the characters themselves lack substance and the plot is thin and frivolous, the centerpiece of the farce is language. Wilde once wrote that the fun of *The Importance of Being Earnest* is in its trivial wit and the charm of the play is in its dialogue. Wilde uses his indefatigable wit and agility of language to take jabs at numerous aspects of life and society, including morality, love, manners, death, decorum, and marriage. The dandies that inhabit the play bear a strong autobiographical connection to the style of Wilde, reflecting the playwright's adamant plea for people to be themselves and do what they want.

Readings on The Importance of Being Earnest is designed to help students gain a greater appreciation of Oscar Wilde's most enduring play. The carefully edited articles provide an overview of the play's ideas, characterization, structure, philosophy, and impact on the world of theater. Each of the literary essays is readable, manageable in length, and focuses on concepts suitable for a beginning exploration into the genre of literary criticism. In addition, this diverse overview of *The Importance of Being Earnest* presents students with a wealth of material for writing reports, designing oral presentations, or enriching their understanding of drama as art.

Oscar Wilde: A Biography

In 1888 the Anglo-Irish poet, novelist, and dramatist Oscar Wilde published a set of fairy stories entitled *The Happy Prince and Other Tales*. Wilde claimed that these stories exercise the reader's capacity for wonder and joy and, like most fairy tales, they present an ordered world where conflicts are resolved happily. But for Wilde the man, the story is very different. His quest to satisfy his considerable sense of wonder and his desire to experience the world according to his nature resulted in anything but a happy ending. The conflicts in which he found himself embroiled ultimately destroyed him. His ending was tragic, driving one of the finest English-speaking thinkers to die dejected and poor in a cheap Parisian hotel, his reputation crushed, his spirit devastated, his health ruined, and his literary output nonexistent.

Wilde was an important and prolific letter writer, a poet of some talent, an essayist, a writer of children's fiction and fantasy, and a superlative playwright. He was also a public speaker who could capture the toughest audiences, even the rough-and-tumble crowds of the western United States; he was a charmer who commanded the attention of some of the most dazzlingly beautiful actresses of his day, including Sarah Bernhardt and Lily Langtry; he was a reformer who campaigned for women's rights and Irish respect; he was an art critic who consistently wrote insightful assessments of art; he was a conversationalist who spoke spontaneously in complete, perfect sentences as if he had meticulously written them out the night before; and he was a piercing wit who effortlessly cranked out epigrams that both amused and provoked his listeners.

Throughout his life he remained an individualist who spoke his mind, unafraid to risk speaking the unpleasant truth in a most pleasant manner. But it was a dangerous game that Wilde played, alternately entertaining and challenging society. Eventually, and perhaps inevitably, powerful elements within society turned on him. He was a homosexual in an age where, in Wilde's words, one "dare not speak its name." Indeed, when Wilde confronted society on this issue, he rapidly found himself hopelessly mired down in sexual scandal. The authorities lashed back and punished him with two years of hard labor, a sentence that ultimately killed him. He emerged from the darkness of the English prison system, moved to France, and lived out his days both bitter and despairing; he was bankrupt, his marriage was dissolved, he was estranged from his children, and he was unable to produce much quality work.

Looking back on his life, he wrote, "I had genius, a distinguished name, high social position, brilliancy, intellectual daring: I altered the minds of men and the colours of things: there was nothing I said or did that did not make people wonder." But in a moment of reflection, he confessed, "I let myself be lured into long spells of senseless and sensual ease. I amused myself with being a *flâneur*, a dandy, a man of fashion. . . . I became the spendthrift of my own genius. . . . I ceased to be Lord over myself. I was no longer Captain of my soul, and did not know it. . . . I ended in horrible disgrace."[1]

CHILDHOOD

Oscar Wilde grew up in an affluent Irish household, shaped by a successful and influential ancestry. The first Wilde to settle in Ireland was a soldier of fortune, Colonel de Wilde, who, because of his military service, was granted land by King William II of England. The colonel's descendants grew to love Ireland, including his grandson Thomas, Oscar's grandfather, who became a respected doctor. Dr. Thomas Wilde, who married into a wealthy and influential family, had three sons. The youngest, William Robert Wills Wilde, became a doctor like his father. William Wilde, Oscar's father, gained a reputation as one of Ireland's finest oculists and surgeons, later receiving the prestigious position of surgeon to Queen Victoria. Not only did he practice medicine successfully, but he also earned respect as an archaeologist who wrote numerous books about Irish folklore.

In 1851 William Wilde married Jane Francesca Elgee. In her young adult years Jane Wilde was an ardent Irish Nationalist who contributed political and revolutionary verse to conservative magazines under the pseudonym Speranza. She gained a fair amount of fame for her passionate support of the Irish fight against English dominance. She not only published several books of poetry, she also wrote essays and translated prose from French and German. After her marriage she settled into family life and focused her writing on Irish folklore. In 1864 Jane Wilde became Lady Jane Wilde when her husband was knighted for his contribution to medicine. This title accentuated her flamboyant personality and her reputation as a social hostess. Known for her exquisite taste and perceptive conversation, Lady Wilde frequently hosted grand dinner parties for leading politicians, poets, and artists. Lady Wilde had a great influence on her son Oscar, who modeled his mother's inquisitive, humorous, and insightful approach to life. She was intensely proud of her son's accomplishments and kept a scrapbook of newspaper clippings focused on Oscar.

Oscar Wilde had two siblings, an older brother, William Wills Wilde, born in 1853, and a younger sister, Isola Francesca, born in 1857. Oscar Fingal O'Flahertie Wills Wilde was born in the family's Dublin home in 1854. When he was just one year old his father's increasing wealth allowed them to move into a large Georgian house, one of the finest in Dublin, and hire a maid, six servants, and a governess, who, along with Lady Wilde, tutored the children at home.

Tragedy struck the Wilde household in 1867 when Isola, a beautiful young girl and the favorite of the entire family, died due to illness. Oscar was deeply affected by his sister's death, and throughout his life he carried a lock of her hair in an envelope with the inscription "She is not dead but sleepeth." When Oscar was ten and his brother twelve, Lady Wilde sent them to Portora Royal School at Enniskillen. At Portora, a public school known for its high academic standards, Oscar's teachers and classmates quickly recognized his giftedness. Oscar told friends later in life that he would make bets with his fellow students that he could read a novel in an hour and present an accurate and detailed account of the plot; a bet that he usually won. Oscar was not popular at Portora, partly because he kept to himself and did not participate in sports or other boyhood games. Although his classmates did not understand him, they were fascinated by his ability to tell stories and humorously imitate the teachers. He did not like mathematics or science, but he passionately loved literature and the classics, especially Greek. Throughout his writing Wilde frequently ridiculed professors and formal education, writing once that "education is an admirable thing, but it is well to remember from time to time that nothing that is worth knowing can be taught."[2]

COLLEGE YEARS

When Wilde was just seventeen, he won a scholarship to a notable Protestant university, Trinity College, in Dublin. Wilde distinguished himself at Trinity. He received several awards for his scholarship in the classics, including the prestigious Berkeley Gold Medal for Greek. He was greatly influenced by two far-reaching intellects: the Reverend J.P. Mahaffy and Robert Yelverton Tyrrell. Tyrrell was a quiet but talented professor of Latin while Mahaffy, the chair of the ancient history department, was an enormous intellect who often flaunted his scholarship. Unfortunately, Mahaffy and Wilde eventually clashed, and the playwright would later satirize the pretentious professor.

In 1872 Willie, Wilde's brother who also attended Trinity, traveled to London to study law. Wilde, twenty years old and anxious for new experiences, also left Trinity after winning a generous scholarship in classics at Oxford University.

Wilde flourished at Oxford. He continually mesmerized his fellow students with his wit, conversation, and extraordinary intellectual and verbal adeptness. While there, he fell under the spell of two extraordinary thinkers: John Ruskin, a renowned art historian, and Walter Pater, the author of *Studies in the History of the Renaissance*, a book that Wilde adored and could quote verbatim. Both scholars taught Wilde the power of art and the necessity of beauty.

This lesson was reinforced in the summer of 1875, when Wilde traveled through Europe with his former teacher J.P. Mahaffy. The beauty of Italy thrilled the impressionable Wilde and the trip seemed to accelerate his growing artistic sensibilities.

Wilde not only gained a reputation as a scholar, but his classmates also knew him as an avid social epicure. He took delight in playing the role of host at lavish college parties, where he polished his art of clever conversation. One Wilde biographer quotes a fellow student who remembered that Wilde "rained paradoxes and laughed at his own absurdities; and after the punch had been drunk, the lights had been put out, the piano had been closed, and most of the guests had gone, there were delightful fireside talks for just Oscar and two or three others."[3]

In 1876 Wilde began to write poetry in earnest, publishing numerous poems in Oxford and Irish periodicals. During his last year at Oxford, Wilde won the university prize for poetry for his poem "Ravenna," named after the city that he grew to love during his tour of Italy. Printed by the university as part of the prize, *Ravenna* was Wilde's first published book. Despite his distinguished student years at college, the school administration surprisingly did not offer Wilde a teaching position. Wilde's future was unresolved: His father had died in April 1876; his mother, after her husband's death, had moved to London; and his brother Willie, who had given up his intention to be a lawyer, was practicing journalism in London. Hence, it was logical that Wilde would move there as well. Disappointed that he did not receive a teaching fellowship, Wilde went to London believing he was beginning a new life, but he was uncertain about the direction it would take. A close friend asked him what he wanted to accomplish there, and the young poet simply stated that he expected to be famous, and if not famous, he believed that he would be notorious.

UNSETTLED YEARS

In London Wilde shared an apartment with an artist and old friend from Oxford, Frank Miles. Miles, a tall, good-looking man who had respectable artistic talent, maintained a studio in one of the rooms, where he was making a name for himself by drawing portraits of the most beautiful women in London. Through the invitations of these women, both Miles and Wilde attended very fashionable parties. Wilde's evening attire was outrageously flamboyant, characterized by velvet coats, bright ties, and silk stockings. It was not long before influential London socialites recognized Wilde as a desirable young aesthete who provided entertaining and meaningful insights into art and beauty. From Wilde's point of view, these early days in London were really part of his overall strategy to attain fame and notoriety.

In 1881, living on a meager income, he received a break with the production of *Patience*, a comic opera satirizing many British customs and traditions written by the famous team of W.S. Gilbert, librettist, and Arthur Sullivan, composer. The producer of the play hired Wilde to promote *Patience* by lecturing in America, which he did with style. Even at the U.S. customs station, Wilde's wit was evident when he stated that he had nothing to declare but his genius. Wilde was a great success in America, and crowds flocked to his lectures and treated him as a star. In a letter that he wrote to the wife of his lawyer, Wilde relishes the success of his lectures in America:

The hall had an audience larger and more wonderful than even [English novelist Charles] Dickens had. I was recalled and applauded and treated like the Royal Boy [the nickname for the Prince of Wales]. I have . . . several secretaries. One writes my autographs all day for my admirers, the other receives the flowers that are left really every ten minutes. A third whose hair resembles mine is obliged to send off locks of his own hair to the myriad maidens of the city, and so is rapidly becoming bald. I stand at the top of the reception rooms when I go out, and for two hours they file past for introduction. I bow graciously and sometimes honour them with a royal observation, which appears next day in all the newspapers.[4]

Wilde learned the trick of promoting himself and he mastered the art of publicity by becoming a public personality.

First Attempts as a Playwright

Wilde continued to write poetry throughout his first years after college, and early in 1881, after being turned down by several publishers, he published a collection of his poems at his own expense. Although he received some encouraging words from the accomplished poet Matthew Arnold, the critics were generally harsh. The cruelest blow came when his alma mater, Oxford, turned down his book of verse for its library.

Convinced that his ability to maintain brilliant and mesmerizing conversation was a skill that would help him write entertaining dramatic dialogue, Wilde turned his artistic attention to writing plays. His first drama, *Vera*, like his collection of poems, did not initially receive favorable attention. However, in 1881 the Adelphi Theatre in London agreed to produce the play. But just as the play was to begin rehearsals, the producer abruptly canceled it. *Vera* centers on events in Russia, and the untimely assassination of Czar Alexander II made the drama politically inappropriate since the czarina was the sister-in-law of England's Prince of Wales.

Wilde's second play, *The Duchess of Padua*, also met with failure. He began writing the play during his 1881 lecture tour of America. He wrote the play with the encouragement and support of a famous American actress, Mary Anderson. But when he finally finished the work in 1883 and sent a copy to her, she responded bluntly that she could not accept the play in its present form, explaining that the part did not fit her. It was not until 1891 that a New York theater staged *The Duchess of Padua* under a different name, *Guido Ferranti*. It failed after only three weeks.

Desperate for money, Wilde agreed in 1883 to a lecture tour of England, arranged by the organizers of his American circuit. Billed as "the Great Aesthete" Wilde's most popular lecture was entitled "Personal Impressions of America."

It was during this time that Wilde met and made friends with the famous painter James McNeill Whistler, himself a notorious wit. The friendship ended in bitterness, however, when the two began to verbally spar with one another. The final blow came when Whistler wrote a letter to the magazine *Truth*, in which he accused Wilde of plagiarizing his ideas. Wilde's rebuttal letter not only refuted Whistler's ideas but also ridiculed the artist's well-known egotism:

> Mr. James Whistler has had the impertinence to attack me with both venom and vulgarity in your columns. I hope you will allow me to state that the assertions contained in his letter are as deliberately untrue as they are deliberately offensive. . . . The only thoroughly original ideas I have ever heard him express have had reference to his own superiority over painters greater than himself. It is a trouble for any gentleman to have to notice the lucubrations [laborious studies] of so ill-bred and ignorant a person as Mr. Whistler.[5]

Wilde's attack resulted in a hostile estrangement between the two men.

The energy spent fighting Whistler, combined with the loneliness of a burdensome lecture tour that eventually caused him to feel like an out-of-place curiosity, made Wilde return to London to recommit himself to writing. The only positive that emerged during the unsettling year of 1883 was Wilde's engagement to Constance Lloyd, a young woman whom he had met two years earlier through a family friend.

CONSTANCE WILDE

On May 29, 1884, Wilde married Lloyd. She was a pretty and talented woman who attended art school, sang, and liked to read. In short, she shared Wilde's interests. In a letter to a friend, Wilde describes his bride-to-be:

> I am going to be married to a beautiful girl called Constance Lloyd, a grave, slight, violet-eyed little Artemis, with great coils of heavy brown hair which make her flower-like head droop like a blo4ssom, and wonderful ivory hands which draw music from the piano so sweet that the birds stop singing to listen to her.[6]

Constance's guardians, her grandparents, left her a small inheritance that supported the couple as Wilde struggled to establish himself as a writer. In the early years of their mar-

riage, Constance was supportive of Wilde's work, often show-
ing up at his lectures wearing unorthodox costumes that reflected her husband's eccentric taste in clothing.

They had two sons: the first, Cyril, was born on June 5,
1885, and the second, Vyvyan, was born on November 5,
1886. Wilde's two sons were a source of joy for him. A close
friend, Frank Harris, records a story that Wilde told that embodies the delight that the playwright took in his sons:

> The other night I [Wilde] was reading when my wife came and
> asked me to go upstairs and reprove the elder boy: Cyril, it ap-
> peared, would not say his prayers. He had quarreled with
> Vyvyan and beaten him, and when he was shaken and told he
> must say his prayers, he would not kneel down, or ask God to
> make him a good boy. Of course I had to go upstairs and see
> to it. I took the chubby little fellow on my knee, and told him
> in a grave way that he had been very naughty; naughty to hit
> his younger brother, and naughty because he had given his
> mother pain. He must kneel down at once, and ask God to for-
> give him and make him a good boy. . . .
>
> "You said you were sorry," questioned his mother, leaning
> over him, "and asked God to make you a good boy?"
>
> "Yes, mother," he nodded. "I said I was sorry and asked God
> to make Vyvyan a good boy."
>
> I had to leave the room, Frank, or he would have seen me
> smiling. Wasn't it delightful of him! We are all willing to ask
> God to make others good.[7]

Although society's expectations for women and the notoriety of her husband often kept Constance in the shadow of
Wilde, she did manage to work for several political causes. She
served as a speaker for a women's suffrage group called the
Women's Liberal Association, which supported the 1888 elec-
tion of Lady Margaret Sandhurst to the London County Council. Constance was also an advocate for a movement in Britain
called the Rational Dress Campaign, which sought to loosen
the restrictive manner in which women were expected to
dress. In an 1888 address to the Rational Dress Society entitled
"Clothed in Our Right Minds," Constance claimed that corsets
and other restrictive clothing worn by Victorian women were
more than uncomfortable, they were dangerous to health and
the necessary freedom of movement. Wilde also wrote on the
subject of fashion. Consistent with his strong sense of individualism and his own unorthodox taste in clothing, he, like Constance, attacked mindless conformity to fashion.

Although frequently absent from the home, Wilde seemed
to relish the outward trappings of a settled family: He and

Constance entertained, visited friends, and went to social functions. Despite the fact that Constance played her public domestic role to perfection, close friends knew that she privately suffered a painful and lonely existence. Wilde spent his energy pursuing his own interests, often directing his love and sexuality outside of the family unit. At times it seemed that Wilde's family was more like a stage setting, with perfectly costumed and positioned actors, than a genuine, loving family. To make matters worse, Wilde's careless management of money, expensive tastes, and boundless generosity frequently kept the household struggling to stay afloat financially.

LIFE AS A JOURNALIST

During the second half of the 1880s, Wilde established himself as a successful journalist and editor. From 1885 to 1887 he wrote art and literary reviews for the *Pall Mall Gazette* and drama critiques for the *Dramatic Review*. In the spring of 1887 the manager of a publishing house asked Wilde to edit a monthly magazine, the *Woman's World*, thus providing Wilde a regular income for the first time in his life. He not only edited the periodical but he also wrote its reviews of literature and art.

Wilde approached journalism with his usual vigor and panache, lacing his articles with precise critical observations and wit. His writing, which covered a wide range of cultural topics, was polished, clever, and filled with quotable insights. Frequently his incisive wit angered or alienated his targets. For example, in a review entitled "Aristotle at Afternoon Tea," Wilde unleashed his satirical voice against his friend, travel companion, and former teacher J.P. Mahaffy.

During this prolific journalistic period Wilde also wrote poetry, a few short stories, and fairy tales published in 1888 as *The Happy Prince and Other Tales*. Although he rarely wrote overtly political pieces, Wilde printed an essay in the *Fortnightly Review* in 1891 entitled "The Soul of Man Under Socialism." With this widely read essay Wilde joined the national debate concerning the credibility and role of socialism. Wilde expressed the notion that the state should eliminate poverty so that individuals would be free to focus their creativity and sense of beauty.

Wilde also published a novel, *The Picture of Dorian Gray*. It first appeared in an American magazine, *Lippincott's Monthly Magazine*, in 1890, and in 1891 a London publishing house printed an expanded version. One of the themes that Wilde explores in *The Picture of Dorian Gray* is the relationship between art and morality. Wilde maintains a position that works of art are neither moral nor immoral; rather, they are simply well done or not well done. The British press attacked the book with extraordinary hostility. They judged it to be a morally poisonous work, potentially dangerous in a Victorian society that guarded an appearance of virtue and standardized moral correctness.

His regular appearance before the public in print and his popular reputation as a flamboyant personality with long flowing hair, extravagant tastes, and eccentric costumes defined Wilde as an idiosyncratic public personality. He and other public figures who sported an aesthetic style were often the talk of London society. The cartoonist George du Maurier satirized Wilde in the popular magazine *Punch* when he introduced a cartoon figure with long hair named Oscuro Wildgoose, sometimes called Drawit Wilde. For years, Wilde was a favorite lampoon target in *Punch* and other publications.

LIFE AS A SUCCESSFUL PLAYWRIGHT

After more than a decade since writing *Vera*, Wilde constructed another play, *Lady Windermere's Fan*. In February 1892 this drama, which Wilde described as a modern drawing-room play, opened in London at the fashionable St. James Theatre, staged by the well-known actor and producer George Alexander. This debut of *Lady Windermere's Fan* initiated a remarkable three-year run for the playwright. A string of five successful plays made Wilde the rightful star of the London drama scene.

Lady Windermere's Fan focuses on a woman who sacrifices herself for her daughter. The play resonated well with audience members, and at the close of the opening performance, they gave the play and its author a standing ovation. Wilde stepped from behind the curtain, smoking a cigarette, and elegantly thanked the stylish audience by saying, "Ladies and Gentlemen. I have enjoyed this evening immensely. The actors have given us a charming rendering of a delightful play, and your appreciation has been most intelligent. I congratulate you on the great success of your performance, which persuades me that you think almost as highly of the play as I do."[8]

Later the same year, Wilde's *Salome*, which he wrote in Paris in 1891, was scheduled to have its London debut at the Palace Theatre starring the beautiful Sarah Bernhardt. After weeks of rehearsal, the cast learned that the play, based on biblical stories, had not received a performance license. All plays in London were required to pass a censorship review according to the Theatres Act of 1843. Works scheduled for public performance had to receive a stamp of approval from the examiner of plays, Lord Chamberlain, and, if necessary, they would be altered to protect the decorum and well-being of the public. *Salome*, which had been staged earlier in Paris, seemed to Lord Chamberlain to be beyond repair, and the controversial play was denied a London performance. It was not until 1894 that *Salome* was translated from its original French into English and was published.

Despite the setback of *Salome*, Wilde soon scored another dramatic victory with *A Woman of No Importance*, produced by Beerbohm Tree at the Haymarket Theatre in April 1893. After spending nearly a month in 1892 at a health spa in Germany to recoup his energy, Wilde returned to England to finish writing the social comedy. The play received an enthusiastic reception from audiences and a generally favorable response from critics. The reviewers found fault with its technical aspects, but they had to admit that they loved watching it. Again Wilde displayed his adept use of language, his indefatigable wit, and his keen understanding of human nature and society. Although the play provided adequate financial resources for Wilde, it did not run as long as *Lady Windermere's Fan*.

In January 1895 Wilde's successful run continued with the opening of *An Ideal Husband* at the Haymarket Theatre. The twists of plot, intrigue, and blackmail in this play delighted the public. It enjoyed an immensely popular run of 111 performances, but it was discontinued when Wilde's name was sullied with a notorious libel case, a situation stemming from a very public accusation that he was having an illegal homosexual affair with the son of a well-known London figure. As with his other successful plays, audiences loved it and critics begrudgingly accepted it. The respectable playwright George Bernard Shaw, writing for the *Saturday Review*, reflected the typical critical opinion when he wrote that the play tricked the audience into frivolity, cleverly getting them to laugh angrily at his epigrams.

THE IMPORTANCE OF BEING EARNEST

During the late summer and fall of 1894 Wilde retreated with his family to the seaside town of Worthing, Sussex, to write his most popular play, *The Importance of Being Earnest.* After just three weeks Wilde was confident that he had a play worthy of staging. In a letter to his friend Lord Alfred Douglas, Wilde exclaimed, "I have been doing nothing here but bathing and playwriting. My play is really very funny: I am quite delighted with it. But it is not shaped yet."[9] Wilde sent his completed comedy to the influential producer George Alexander for review, writing in his cover letter, "It is called *Lady Lancing* on the cover: but the real title is *The Importance of Being Earnest.* When you read the play, you will see the punning title's meaning."[10] Alexander rejected it but suggested it would play better if Wilde cut it from four acts to three. Wilde reworked the play in three acts, removing a lengthy scene concerning debt collection. At the time, bailiffs who wanted money for his outstanding debts were pursuing the playwright.

Oscar Wilde

Fortunately for Wilde, the play that Alexander was staging at his popular St. James Theatre failed miserably and the producer closed it abruptly. After a number of alterations, Alexander agreed to stage Wilde's revised comedy, and after rushed and often frantic rehearsals, it opened a month later on February 14, 1895, with Alexander playing Jack Worthing. In a pre–opening night newspaper interview, a reporter asked the playwright if the play would be a success, to which Wilde deftly responded, "My dear fellow, you have got it all wrong. The play *is* a success. The only question is whether the first night's audience will be one."[11] Despite terrible winter weather and one postponed opening night due to illness, the initial performance drew a full house. The play was a sensation; the audience rose to its feet at its conclusion and cheered wildly. The actor who played Algernon Moncrieff later stated that, in fifty-three years of acting, he had never seen such an overwhelmingly triumphant opening performance.

The critics of 1895 generally wrote favorable reviews of *Earnest.* One reviewer captured the reaction of the audience when he wrote, "It is delightful to see, it sends wave after wave of laughter curling and foaming round the theatre."[12]

However, the drama also drew criticism. Some reviewers felt that the play relied far too heavily on verbal pyrotechnics and that the wit frequently went annoyingly overboard. Others complained that the play lacked meaning and that Wilde's style was affected and contrived. Again, George Bernard Shaw led the charge:

> It amused me, of course; but unless comedy touches me as well as amuses me, it leaves me with a sense of having wasted my evening. I go to the theatre to be moved to laughter, not to be tickled or bustled into it; and this is why, though I laugh as much as anybody at a farcical comedy, I am out of spirits before the end of the second act, and out of temper before the end of the third.[15]

Still others felt uncomfortable with the characters, claiming they were nothing more than vague vehicles to spout clever epigrams.

The play had run for a full month, enjoying full houses for each performance, when, on April 5, 1895, authorities arrested Oscar Wilde. His arrest and subsequent trial caused Alexander, acquiescing to societal prudery, to remove the playwright's name from the playbill and all advertising. *The Importance of Being Earnest* continued for one more month, but to smaller audiences. It ran for a total of eighty-one performances before Alexander shut it down, resulting in a loss of revenues. Today, of course, playgoers consider Wilde's farce to be one of the funniest ever written. Audiences around the world find something in the play that resonates with their experiences in society.

SEXUALITY

In 1886, at age thirty-two, Wilde met Robert Ross, the seventeen-year-old grandson of the governor general of Canada, and the two became lovers and friends for life. Whether Wilde's liaisons with Ross were his first homosexual experiences is hard to tell since many of his closest friends at Oxford and throughout his early adulthood were homosexuals. Nevertheless, Wilde's predilection for young men would be the vehicle for the tragedy of his life: his downfall and ultimate two-year imprisonment as a sodomite.

In England at that time it was illegal to practice homosexuality. Perhaps it is more accurate to say that one could be found guilty of homosexuality if one did not keep one's private life to oneself. Wilde, however, made his sexuality, like so many other aspects of his life, a matter of public record.

The homosexual relationship that finally destroyed Wilde was with Lord Alfred Douglas, the third son of the eighth marquess of Queensberry. Wilde met Douglas, sixteen years Wilde's junior, in 1891 while Wilde was visiting his former college, Magdalen, where Douglas was enrolled as a student. Wilde fell desperately in love with this young man, who was known for his good looks and his poetic ability. Douglas, nicknamed Bosie, returned Wilde's affection, and the two, despite many bitter quarrels and spats, became lovers. In a letter to his friend and former lover, Robert Ross, Wilde exclaims his passion for the young Bosie:

> My Dearest Bobbie, Bosie has insisted on stopping here for sandwiches. He is quite like a narcissus—so white and gold. I will come either Wednesday or Thursday night to your rooms. Send me a line. Bosie is so tired: he lies like a hyacinth on the sofa, and I worship him.
>
> You dear boy. Ever yours, Oscar.[14]

The two spent much of their time together, and Wilde spent vast amounts of money entertaining the young man, often pushing his personal finances to the brink of ruin.

Douglas's father, a rather abrupt, mean-spirited man who no longer lived with his wife and son, heard of the Wilde relationship and demanded that Douglas break it off. Lord Queensberry was known as a forceful man who had made a reputation in the world of boxing as a successful promoter and initiator of a set of boxing regulations called the Queensberry rules. At one point Lord Queensberry told his son directly that his "intimacy with this man Wilde must either cease or I will disown you."[15] In response, Douglas wired his father with the terse message, "What a funny little man you are."[16] The elder Douglas, enraged, increased his demands to the point of threatening both his son and Wilde with physical violence. In an effort to confront Wilde, Lord Queensberry left a visiting card at Wilde's mens' club in which he directly accused Wilde of posing as a sodomite. Shocked at Lord Queensberry's breach of etiquette and perhaps frightened, Wilde wrote a prophetic letter to Robert Ross: "Since I last saw you something has happened—Bosie's father has left a card at my Club with hideous words on it. I don't see anything now but a criminal prosecution—my whole life seems ruined by this man."[17] At one point Lord Queensberry's rage boiled to such a point that he and a prizefighter escort showed up at the 1895 opening night performance of *The Importance of Being Earnest*, intending to disrupt the play by shouting insults and throwing rotten vegetables on stage. Fortunately, the police stopped him at the door.

Encouraged by Douglas, who wanted desperately to see his father humiliated, Wilde hired solicitor Sir Edward Clarke to prosecute Lord Queensberry for libel. Clarke had a solid reputation for taking cases in which he was sure that his client was innocent. When Clarke asked Wilde if Queensberry's charges were true, Wilde responded by saying unequivocally that they were not. Perhaps if Wilde had answered honestly, Clarke would have dropped the case and helped Wilde avoid the tragedy that was about to unfold.

Unfortunately for Wilde, his homosexual activities were well known by a rather substantial group of people in London. In fact, several very damaging letters written by Wilde to his lover were in the hands of potential blackmailers. It turns out that Douglas had given one of his suits to a young man he had been seeing, not realizing that Wilde's letters were still in the pocket. The momentum turned against Wilde. Queensberry hired a brilliant barrister, Edward Carson, who, ironically, had been a friend and classmate of Wilde's at Trinity College. Carson quickly aligned numerous witnesses to attest to Wilde's homosexual behavior.

At the time, Wilde received conflicting advice. Many of his friends, realizing that Wilde was facing a serious situation that he would probably lose, told him to drop the charges and let the situation cool down by leaving the country for a while. Contrarily, Alfred Douglas, blinded by his own self-centeredness and motivated by a consuming drive to hurt his father, urged Wilde to continue with the libel case.

In the witness box, Wilde was his usual brilliant self, answering questions with wit and aplomb. But the evidence was stacked against him, and it quickly became apparent that Wilde's charge of libel was unfounded because the playwright was indeed a homosexual. After three days of trial, Clarke withdrew as counsel and Wilde lost his case. Queensberry now felt justified, and he went on the offensive by obtaining a warrant for Wilde's arrest. Despite the impending calamity, Wilde had an opportunity to take a train to France and thereby avoid the arrest warrant, but he refused. With the urging of his lawyer, Douglas fled to Europe just before the start of Wilde's trial.

Wilde stood alone facing twenty-five charges of gross indecency according to the Criminal Law Amendment Act of 1885, which allowed the courts to imprison someone for homosexual acts. From the stand Wilde denied all charges of indecency, claiming that he was fascinated by youth but that he had done nothing indecent. On May 1, 1895, the jury could not agree on a verdict, so the judge scheduled a second trial to begin on May 20. The public was both shocked and fascinated as the details of the two trials were reported in the newspapers, bringing homosexuality into the public domain for the first time.

The jury found Wilde guilty, and the judge sentenced him to two years of hard labor at the harsh Reading Gaol prison. Wilde later described his first days of incarceration to his friend Frank Harris:

> The cell was appalling: I could hardly breathe in it, and the food turned my stomach; the smell and sight of it were enough: I did not eat anything for days and days and days, I could not even swallow the bread; and the rest of the food was uneatable; I lay on the so-called bed and shivered all night long. . . . After some days I got so hungry I had to eat a little, nibble at the outside of the bread, and drink some of the liquid; whether it was tea, coffee or gruel, I could not tell. As soon as I really ate anything it produced violent diarrhea and I was ill all day and all night. From the beginning I could not sleep, I grew weak and had wild delusions. . . . The hunger made you weak; but the inhumanity was the worst of it. What devilish creatures men are. I had never known anything about them. I had never dreamt of such cruelties.[18]

During his two years of hard labor, Wilde suffered immensely: He lost his health, he anguished mentally and psychologically, he was divorced, he went bankrupt, and he lost his esteem in the eye of the public. The absence of common everyday amenities were the hardest to bear for the playwright: conversation, books, and writing paper. His name was so anathema that his wife and children, traveling in Switzerland under a false name, were required to leave a hotel when it became known who they were.

While in prison Wilde's alienation was compounded when he heard the news that his mother had died at the beginning of 1896. Wilde's affection for his mother ran very deep and her death added to his sense of isolation:

> No one knew how deeply I loved and honoured her. Her death was terrible to me; but I, once a lord of language, have no words in which to express my anguish and my shame. She and my father had bequeathed me a name they had made noble and honoured, not merely in literature, art, archaeology, and science, but in the public history of my own country, in its evolution as a nation. I had disgraced that name eternally.[19]

The news was delivered by his wife, the first contact she had with her husband since the beginning of the libel trial and, as it turns out, the only face-to-face contact the two would ever have again. Wilde was unsuccessful with his petitions to have his sentence reduced. Only toward the end of his imprisonment was he allowed to have a limited supply of paper. Wilde felt abandoned in prison; friends who he was sure would continue to support him never did, particularly Douglas, who traveled through Europe. Wilde came to realize the selfishness that drove Douglas, and he suffered the humiliation of knowing that his actions had been manipulated by his young lover's hatred for his father.

In a long letter written in 1897, just before his release from prison, Wilde blamed Douglas for his downfall. The letter, actually a long essay later entitled "De Profundis," chastises Douglas for his neglectful behavior, but it also beautifully presents an autobiographical look into the feelings of Wilde as an artist. In "De Profundis" the playwright and poet elegantly elaborates on his inner strength, his role as a victim of society, the nobility of suffering, and the functioning of an artistic mind. Widely distributed before World War I, "De Profundis" is one of the finest essays written in English and did a great deal to restore Wilde's literary reputation.

THE YEARS AFTER PRISON

Upon his release from prison, Wilde's longtime friend Robert Ross helped the frail playwright get resettled. Wilde assumed the name Sebastian Melmoth and moved to Dieppe, France, never to return to England again. The name of Melmoth was based on a character from a play, *Melmoth the Wanderer*, written by Wilde's great uncle Charles Robert Maturin. Eventually Wilde's strength returned enough that he began to write poetry again, creating his last serious work, *The Ballad of Reading Gaol.* This ballad explores the pain of prisoners as they suffer the last days with a condemned inmate, a soldier who killed his wife. Although the poem did not rejuvenate Wilde's literary career when he was alive, it is considered posthumously as one of his most movingly written poems.

Despite his bitterness toward Lord Alfred Douglas and the fact that Constance had threatened to cut off his financial support if he ever saw Douglas again, Wilde gave in to Douglas's persistent requests and agreed to see his former lover. Unable to overcome his counterproductive passion for Douglas, Wilde seemingly reconciled with the younger man and they traveled throughout Italy together. Outraged, Constance refused to see Wilde herself or to allow him to visit their sons. Then, in April 1898, Wilde learned that Constance, age forty, had died of complications from a spinal operation. Wilde was overwhelmed by the unexpected news of her death: "It is awful. I don't know what to do. If we had only met once and kissed each other. It is too late. How awful life is." [20] Wilde visited her grave and was hurt that her family had chosen to omit Wilde from her name on the tombstone:

> It was very tragic seeing her name carved on a tomb, her sur-name—my name not mentioned of course—just "Constance Mary, daughter of Horace Lloyd, Q.C." and a verse from Revelations. I bought some flowers. I was deeply affected, with a sense, also, of the uselessness of all regrets. Nothing could have been otherwise, and life is a very terrible thing. [21]

For the rest of the year Wilde wandered around France, Italy, and Switzerland, sometimes with Douglas, sometimes with Ross, and often alone.

Eventually Wilde settled into an apartment at the inexpensive Hotel d'Alsace in Paris. Living off the modest money left to him by Constance, Wilde was pressed financially. Many of his former friends neglected him financially, including Douglas, whom Wilde had earlier showered with gifts and money.

In the middle months of 1900 Wilde suffered progressively severe headaches. An attending doctor hastily recommended an ear operation that left Wilde in great pain and in need of a full-time attendant. Cognizant that he might be dying, Wilde telegraphed his faithful friend Robert Ross, requesting that he come immediately, writing, "Terribly weak. Please come." Poor and dying, Wilde quipped from his deathbed, "I am dying beyond my means. I will never outlive the century. The English people would not stand for it." [22] On November 30, 1900, Wilde died comforted by Ross and a few other friends. Just before his death, Wilde received his last rites after becoming a deathbed convert to the Roman Catholic Church.

The *New York Times* ran a full-column front-page story announcing Oscar Wilde's death. Under the heading "Death of Oscar Wilde," a subheading read, "He expires at an obscure hotel in the Latin Quarter of Paris. Is said to have died from meningitis, but there is a rumor that he committed suicide." [23] This simple and speculative newspaper subhead seems to encapsulate the public watchfulness that defined Wilde's life: fascination laced with awe, misinformation, and misunderstanding. Wilde was a master of self-dramatization, inexorably drawing the public's eye to his original and brilliant mind and his self-generated, flamboyant, and nearly mythical persona. He regularly appeared in magazines, often parodied; he was a flimsily disguised character in several published works; and he was the topic of numerous songs, such as the comic tune written by M.H. Rosenfeld entitled "Dear Oscar," or the dance number called the "Oscar Polka Mazurka," which contained the choral refrain "Oscar dear, Oscar dear, How fluttery, utterly flutter you are, Oscar dear, Oscar dear, I think you are awfully 'wild,' ta! ta!"[24]

In short, Oscar Wilde's life, like his plays, drew an audience, entertained, and provoked people to see society and themselves differently. Reflecting on the life of his friend, Frank Harris later wrote, "Oscar Wilde's greatest play was his own life. It was a five-act tragedy with Greek implications and he was its most ardent spectator."[25]

Douglas rushed to Paris upon hearing the news of Wilde's illness, but he arrived too late to see him alive. Wilde is buried in a cemetery in Paris. His tombstone has a quote from *The Ballad of Reading Gaol*:

And alien tears will fill for him
Pity's long broken urn
For his mourners will be outcast men
And outcasts always mourn.[26]

NOTES

1. Oscar Wilde, *Selected Letters of Oscar Wilde*, ed. Rupert Hart-Davis. Oxford, England: Oxford University Press, 1979, p. 194.
2. Quoted in Philippe Jullian, *Oscar Wilde*. London: Constable, 1969, p. 21.
3. Louis Kronenberger, *Oscar Wilde*. Boston: Little, Brown, 1976, p. 19.
4. Wilde, *Selected Letters of Oscar Wilde*, p. 31.
5. Wilde, *Selected Letters of Oscar Wilde*, p. 80.
6. Quoted in Jullian, *Oscar Wilde*, p. 137.
7. Quoted in Frank Harris, *Oscar Wilde*. East Lansing: Michigan State University Press, 1959, p. 104.
8. Quoted in Michael Hardwick, *The Osprey Guide to Oscar Wilde*. Berkshire, England: Osprey, 1973, p. 179.
9. Wilde, *Selected Letters of Oscar Wilde*, p. 120.

10. Wilde, *Selected Letters of Oscar Wilde*, p. 125.
11. Quoted in Hardwick, *The Osprey Guide to Oscar Wilde*, p. 215.
12. Quoted in Hardwick, *The Osprey Guide to Oscar Wilde*, p. 215.
13. Quoted in Hardwick, *The Osprey Guide to Oscar Wilde*, p. 215.
14. Quoted in Richard Ellmann, *Oscar Wilde*. New York: Alfred A. Knopf, 1988, p. 385.
15. Quoted in Kronenberger, *Oscar Wilde*, p. 136.
16. Quoted in Boris Brasol, *Oscar Wilde: The Man, the Artist, the Martyr*. New York: Charles Scribner's Sons, 1938, p. 234.
17. Quoted in Brasol, *Oscar Wilde*, p. 251.
18. Quoted in H. Montgomery Hyde, *Oscar Wilde: The Aftermath*. New York: Farrar, Straus, 1963, p. 5.
19. Quoted in Robert Harborough Sherard, *The Life of Oscar Wilde*. New York: Dodd, Mead, 1928, p. 6.
20. Quoted in Hyde, *Oscar Wilde*, p. 182.
21. Quoted in Hyde, *Oscar Wilde*, p. 182.
22. Quoted in Ellmann, *Oscar Wilde*, p. 580.
23. Karl Beckson, ed., *Oscar Wilde: The Critical Heritage*. London: Routledge & Kegan Paul, 1970, p. 225.
24. Quoted in Anne Varty, *A Preface to Oscar Wilde*. London: Addison Wesley Longman, 1988, p. 37.
25. Quoted in M.H. Abrams, ed., *The Norton Anthology of English Literature*, vol. 2. New York: W.W. Norton, 1962, p. 1214.
26. Oscar Wilde, *The Ballad of Reading Gaol*. London: Gerald Duckworth, 1997, p. 73.

CHARACTERS AND PLOT

CHARACTERS

Although the critical responses to *The Importance of Being Earnest* were essentially favorable, the reviewers did frequently criticize Wilde's characterization. They complained that the characters were exaggerated, unnatural, or inauthentic. Some critics suggested that all of the characters really represented just one voice, Wilde's.

The characters in the play are types whose clever talk takes precedence over the flow of the plot. Frequently Wilde will stop the action of the story so a character can display his verbal cleverness and wit. The audience cannot expect to delve deep into the soul of the characters because they are surface creatures. Moreover, the audience cannot expect to learn much about the characters from their interplay with each other because they rarely interact in a meaningful manner. In short, they do not really develop internally; they simply react to external events. Wilde does not intend his characters to be realistic, psychologically complex, emotionally moving, or subtly evolving. They are the players in a farce, artificial and affected, inhabiting a world where language is more important than character.

Jack Worthing. Jack Worthing is the adopted son of Thomas Cardew and the guardian of Cardew's granddaughter, Cecily Cardew. Worthing, like his brother Algernon Moncrieff, is a dandy who is self-absorbed, finely dressed, and uses language and wit to compete with others. The critic Eric Bentley suggests that Worthing and the other characters wear savoir faire masks as a means to protect themselves from modern society. Worthing, again like Moncrieff, invents a fictional character to make it easier for him to do as he pleases. This duality is reflected also in his personality: Worthing, like the other young lovers in the play, displays an inconsistency between his surface polish and the innocence and incognizance of his behavior. Much of the play's humor arises from this incongruous interaction of opposites, in which the characters react to serious situations with a surprisingly trivial or naive response.

In the original production of *The Importance of Being Earnest*, the actor and producer George Alexander played Jack Worthing. A review of Alexander's acting appeared in the publication *Era* shortly after opening night:

> George Alexander played Worthing just as a part of this sort should be played, i.e., with entire seriousness and no indication of purposed irony. He never once ceased to realize that the effect of the author's conception in a piece of this kind is marred immediately that the artists appear to see the fun.[1]

Algernon Moncrieff. Algernon Moncrieff is the nephew of Lady Bracknell and the first cousin of Gwendolen Fairfax. It turns out from the astonishing revelations at the end of the play that Moncrieff is the brother of Jack Worthing. Moncrieff is a conceited ladies' man who uses language and wit to promote himself and dominate others. Like Worthing, Moncrieff has invented a fictitious friend, named Bunbury, so that he can escape whenever he feels the need. His deceit, like Worthing's, weakens his credibility as a person of earnestness. At one point even Worthing complains to Lady Bracknell about her nephew, "I do not approve at all of his moral character. I suspect him of being untruthful."

Moncrieff is committed to pleasure and fulfilling his desires. This is best represented in his voracious appetite. When he eats all of the cucumber sandwiches laid out for tea, the audience symbolically witnesses his dominant character trait—his sensuality and sexual desire.

Gwendolen Fairfax. Gwendolen Fairfax is Lady Bracknell's daughter and the first cousin of Algernon Moncrieff. She is the product of London's high society: fashionable, self-absorbed, and sophisticated. She is very much aware of how she appears; everything she says is preconceived and done for effect. She is not only a product of the city, uninterested in the unsophisticated isolation of country life, but she is also the product of manufactured and practiced social interaction. For example, when she believes that she and Cecily Cardew are betrothed to the same man, she skillfully and effortlessly shifts to a demeanor of aggressive politeness and cold social formality.

Like Lady Bracknell, she speaks from unfailing authority: "I never change except in my affections." Moncrieff warns that Fairfax's tragedy will result from the fact that she will become like her mother.

Cecily Cardew. Cecily Cardew is the granddaughter of the deceased Thomas Cardew and the ward of Jack Worthing. She is a pretty eighteen-year-old who, despite growing up in the country, cannot only match, but usually top, the clever verbal repartee fired by the caustic Gwendolen Fairfax. Although she seems less artificial than Fairfax, she is nevertheless as manipulative and cunning.

Cardew keeps a journal laced with sensual entries in which she has written love letters from an imaginary lover named Ernest. Despite being self-assured on the surface, Cardew, like the other characters, is innocent just below the surface.

Miss Laetitia Prism. Miss Laetitia Prism is Cecily Cardew's governess and the former nursemaid for Jack Worthing, or Ernest Moncrieff, as he was named at the time. She presents the mask of Victorian respectability, quick to moralize and make judgmental pronouncements. It is interesting to note that this symbol of society's rules and morals is the very person who neglected the younger generation when she lost the baby Ernest Moncrieff. Nevertheless, despite her old-fashioned views, there is beneath her outer personality an active sensuality and sexual desire for Dr. Chasuble. This urge is presumably rewarded at the end of the play when she embraces the doctor of divinity and exclaims, "Frederick! At last!"

Lady Bracknell. Lady Bracknell is the mother of Gwendolen Fairfax and the aunt of Algernon Moncrieff. She married into the privileged class and has taken to the role wonderfully. She is inflexible, snobbish, self-righteous, and unswervingly materialistic. When interviewing Jack Worthing as a possible suitor for Fairfax, she gets right to the point by asking him how much money he makes. When Worthing reveals a respectable figure, she immediately changes her perspective of him. At one point, Worthing describes Lady Bracknell as a gorgon: "She is a monster, without being a myth, which is rather unfair." She is never at a loss to provide unsolicited pronouncements about the order and structure of society:

> I do not approve of anything that tampers with natural ignorance. Ignorance is like a delicate exotic fruit; touch it and the bloom is gone. The whole theory of modern education is radically unsound. Fortunately in England, at any rate, education

produces no effect whatsoever. If it did, it would prove a serious danger to the upper classes and probably lead to acts of violence.

Lady Bracknell's perspective of education, like many of her other absurd opinions, is built on an emotionless perspective that is steadfastly superficial and void of thoughtfulness.

Lady Bracknell plays a pivotal role in the play, serving as the roadblock that prevents the marriages of the young lovers. She also serves as the deus ex machina when she suddenly provides the unexpected and unbelievable information to clarify Worthing's seemingly insoluble family shortcoming: Worthing is the son of her sister, Mrs. Moncrieff, and therefore the elder brother of Algernon. With Worthing's lineage in place, he fits Lady Bracknell's requirements for a suitable son-in-law.

THE PLOT

After the opening performance of *The Importance of Being Earnest*, a drama critic for the *Times* wrote, "Whether in farce or drama, plot continues to be Mr. Oscar Wilde's most vulnerable point. The story of this latest production is, indeed, almost too preposterous to go without music."[2] Nevertheless, audiences overwhelmingly enjoyed the preposterousness of the play, thoroughly relishing its farcical plot. Wilde generates amusement by exploiting exaggerated situations, incongruities, reversals of relationships, witty expressions, and ludicrous twists of fate. He cleverly weaves them together in a story line of mistaken identity, idiosyncratic characters, and plot twists that seemingly defy logic. The result is a very humorous play that draws the audience into a compelling comedic world where absurdity and wit are the unifying threads of the drama.

ACT I

Act 1 begins with the meeting of two friends: John "Jack" Worthing and Algernon Moncrieff. Worthing, who lives in the country, enters Moncrieff's London apartment to announce his intention to marry Moncrieff's first cousin, Gwendolen Fairfax. As Worthing enters the flat, the butler, Lane, announces the visitor as Mr. Ernest Worthing. Worthing explains that he calls himself "Ernest" because he has assumed two personas: In the country he remains Jack, a responsible and down-to-earth character, but in the city he is Ernest, a character who is dissolute and unrestrained.

Worthing pretends that the two selves are brothers, which gives him a good excuse to go to the city or return to the country. Worthing's duality does not come as a complete surprise to Moncrieff because he had discovered Worthing's lost cigarette case left behind on an earlier visit. The case is inscribed with the statement "To Ernest, from little Cecily with her fondest love." When pressed by Moncrieff, Worthing confesses that Miss Cecily Cardew is his ward, who, along with her governess, Miss Laetitia Prism, lives at Worthing's country home. Worthing reveals that Cardew's grandfather, Mr. Thomas Cardew, a wealthy estate owner who had adopted Worthing as an infant, stipulated in his will that Worthing assume the role of Cardew's guardian upon the old man's death. Moncrieff, who has earned a reputation as a fashionable lady's man, expresses an interest in meeting Cardew, but Worthing, in order to protect his ward, refuses to tell Moncrieff the exact location of his country home.

Moncrieff confesses that he too has an imaginary personality that he calls Bunbury. Unlike Algernon, who radiates health and exuberance, the Bunbury alter ego is a permanent invalid. Having a sickly fictional friend like Bunbury allows Moncrieff a perfect excuse to escape into the country for badly needed rest and quietness, a tactic that Moncrieff calls "Bunburying." When Moncrieff suggests that both he and Worthing are dedicated "Bunburyists," Worthing exclaims emphatically that he will gladly let go of Ernest when Gwendolen Fairfax agrees to marry him.

At this point, Fairfax and her mother, Lady Bracknell, enter the apartment. When Lady Bracknell and Moncrieff retire to the music room to practice music for a reception, Worthing takes the opportunity to tell Fairfax that he admires her more than any other woman. Fairfax, who knows Jack as Ernest, responds by admitting that Worthing has always been an irresistible fascination for her. She explains that there is something in the name *Ernest* that "inspires absolute confidence" and that "the moment that Moncrieff first mentioned to me that he had a friend called Ernest, I knew I was destined to love you." Amazed that the name *Ernest* has such a power over Fairfax, Worthing tests his actual name, suggesting that *Jack* might really be a better name than *Ernest*. Fairfax rejects the name *Jack* and its more formal form, *John*, as charmless. Despite the falsehood surrounding his name, Jack Worthing proposes and Fairfax accepts.

When Lady Bracknell returns and learns of the engagement, she presents Worthing with a series of questions to determine whether she will accept the engagement. In the process of questioning, Worthing reveals that he does not know his parents and that as an infant he was found in a handbag at Victoria Station by the late Mr. Thomas Cardew who gave him the name of Worthing because the child had a first-class ticket for Worthing, Sussex, in his pocket at the time. Lady Bracknell argues that "to be born . . . in a handbag . . . seems to me to display contempt for the ordinary decencies of family life that reminds one of the worst excesses of the French Revolution." She rejects the engagement and strongly recommends that Worthing produce at least one parent, of either sex, before the season is over. After Lady Bracknell exits the room, Fairfax returns briefly to tell Worthing that, despite her mother, she remains devoted to him and asks for his country address, which Moncrieff overhears and surreptitiously writes down on his shirt cuff.

Act II

The second act takes place in the country at the Worthing Manor House. In the garden eighteen-year-old Cecily Cardew receives a German lesson from her governess, Miss Prism. Questioning from Cardew reveals that Prism had written, but subsequently lost, a long multivolume manuscript for a novel. Their conversation is interrupted when Prism's admirer, the Reverend Dr. Chasuble arrives and the two depart for a leisurely walk. The butler informs Cardew that Worthing's brother, Ernest, has just arrived from the city, and since Jack is not at home, he desires to speak with her. Worthing led Cardew to believe that his fictitious brother, Ernest, her cousin, is a wicked and ominous man, and she is therefore surprised to find that Moncrieff, posing as Ernest, is really very handsome and refined. Cardew encourages him to stay at the manor until Worthing returns. After they exit, Prism and Chasuble enter in time to meet Worthing returning from London, dressed in funeral black. He explains that his brother has died, and he unexpectedly asks the reverend to christen him as Ernest that very afternoon.

Cardew and Moncrieff return, holding hands, and Cardew informs Worthing that his brother indeed has redeemable qualities, such as taking tender care of his invalid friend Bunbury. When they are alone, Worthing demands that the imposter Moncrieff leave immediately. Before leaving, Moncrieff, still posing as Ernest, asks Cardew to marry him and she accepts, declaring that she had been enamored with him for three months before meeting him because of his charming name, Ernest. Like Gwendolen Fairfax, Cecily Cardew is determined to marry a man named Ernest. After Moncrieff scurries off to find the minister, the plot grows more complex when the butler announces that Fairfax has arrived to see Mr. Worthing. Despite the fact that the two women like one another, tension arises when their conversation reveals that they are both engaged to Ernest Worthing.

Suddenly Worthing enters and Fairfax endearingly calls him Ernest. When Moncrieff returns to the garden, Fairfax and Cardew discover the truth. There are two pairs of lovers, two men who have claimed to be Ernest, and no actual Ernest. The women move from the garden into the house, united as friends by the deception.

ACT III

The third act takes place in the Worthing Manor House drawing room, where Fairfax and Cardew await an explanation from Worthing and Moncrieff. When the two men exclaim that they are willing to have their names changed to satisfy their lovers, the couples are reconciled. This is short-lived, however, when Lady Bracknell enters the room. Not only does Lady Bracknell continue to object to Worthing's background, but she also disapproves of her nephew, Moncrieff, intending to marry Cardew. When Worthing informs Lady Bracknell that Cardew has a fortune of £130,000, she quickly changes her position: "Miss Cardew seems to me a most attractive young lady, now that I look at her." Despite Lady Bracknell's approval, Worthing, as Cardew's guardian, disapproves of his ward's marriage to Moncrieff. Worthing suggests that Moncrieff can have his blessing to marry Cardew if Lady Bracknell approves of his marriage to Fairfax. Lady Bracknell refuses, holding to her earlier requirement that Worthing produce a worthy family lineage.

Just as Lady Bracknell and her nephew are about to depart, Dr. Chasuble enters to perform the christening. In his conversation he refers to Miss Prism, and upon hearing the name, Lady Bracknell is taken by surprise. After Prism is summoned, Lady Bracknell explains that twenty-eight years ago Prism was the nursemaid at Lord Bracknell's estate. On one eventful day, Prism took the baby in a carriage and her novel manuscript in a handbag and, according to Prism, suffered an unexplained mental lapse when she "deposited the manuscript in the basinette, and placed the baby in the hand-bag," forgetting it at the Victoria railway station. After Prism confirms that Worthing's handbag is indeed the one left at the station, Lady Bracknell informs Worthing that he is the son of her sister, Mrs. Moncrieff, and, most surprisingly, the elder brother of Algernon Moncrieff. She concludes that Worthing's christened name, which she had forgotten, would be the same as his father, Ernest John Moncrieff. Worthing asserts, "I always told you, Gwendolen, my name was Ernest, didn't I? Well, it is Ernest after all. I mean it naturally is Ernest." Worthing pleads with Gwendolen Fairfax to forgive him for suddenly speaking the truth, and he concludes the play with the statement, "I've now realised for the first time in my life the vital Importance of Being Earnest."

NOTES

1. Quoted in Robert Tanitch, *Oscar Wilde on Stage and Screen.* London: Methuen, 1999, p. 259.
2. Quoted in Tanitch, *Oscar Wilde on Stage and Screen,* p. 258.

CHAPTER 1

Wilde's Use of Language in *The Importance of Being Earnest*

READINGS ON
THE IMPORTANCE
OF BEING EARNEST

The Importance of Being Earnest as a Verbal Opera

Alan Bird

The English literary critic Alan Bird agrees with the
poet and dramatist W.H. Auden that *The Importance
of Being Earnest* is a verbal opera. According to Bird,
Wilde's play, like the comic operas of Gilbert and Sullivan, sacrifices the dramatic elements to allow the
full range of "arias" in the form of clever dialogue.
Bird also contends that, like an opera, the construction of the play rests on secrets that move the plot
with involved schemes of deception and deceit. All
the characters work diligently and cleverly to avoid
disclosure of the scandals in their lives. Bird writes
that these elements of deception, and the resulting
misunderstandings, form the basis of good farce.

Bird argues that Wilde, like Shakespeare, finds a
redemptive quality in love and marriage. At their
marriages, both John and Algernon "kill off" their
false personas and begin a new married life. This
transformation is parallel to a baptism or a christening at which the characters find redemption, a new
state of earnestness. Bird also maintains that eating
and drinking, which are continuous throughout the
play, are used meaningfully as a symbol of social
and personal status. Although the rigid English class
system is present in the play, Wilde's humor reflects
a genuine affection for his acquisitive and snobbish
characters.

Contemporary critics stressed Wilde's indebtedness to the
French theatre and to Beaumarchais [French dramatist, assumed name of Pierre Augustin Caron] among other writers
of comedy—they would have done better to have mentioned

[French dramatist Eugene] Labiche whose *Celimaire* has some similarities with *The Importance of Being Earnest;* they also mentioned the influence of [English dramatist and librettist William Schwenck] W.S. Gilbert and whether they meant Gilbert the dramatist or Gilbert the librettist is unimportant because in both capacities he was deservedly famous for his neat, farcical constructions. [English poet and dramatist, Wystan Hugh] W.H. Auden states:

> in 'The Importance of Being Earnest' Wilde succeeded—almost, it would seem, by accident, for he never realised its infinite superiority to all his other plays—in writing what is perhaps the only pure verbal opera in English. The solution that, deliberately or accidentally, he found was to subordinate every other dramatic element to dialogue for its own sake and create a verbal universe in which the characters are determined by the kinds of things they say, and the plot is nothing but a succession of opportunities to say them.

Auden seems here to have put his finger on a basic element in this comedy, although he does less than justice to the visual factors and to Wilde's sense of social justice which pervades the greater part of his work. Nevertheless, *The Importance of Being Earnest* can reasonably be described as a purely verbal opera, with all the fun and gaiety to be found in the comic operas of Gilbert and [English composer Sir Arthur] Sullivan but without any of the pathos or sympathetic studies of love to be found in those of [Austrian composer Wolfgang Amadeus] Mozart. The play falls, as most producers from Alexander onward have realised, into set pieces: duets, trios, quartets, and septets, as well as into a number of arias of a varied and baroque nature. Even the amusing mistake, vastly improbable as it was, whereby Jack Worthing, when a baby, was placed in a hand-bag and deposited in the cloak-room at Victoria Station and the manuscript of a three-decker novel put in his place in the basinette by the absent-minded Miss Prism has its counterpart in opera, serious and comic. The hero of *The Pirates of Penzance* when a boy was mistakenly apprenticed to a pirate instead of a pilot; and Azucena in *Il Trovatore* more tragically but hardly less improbably throws the wrong baby into the fire. The fact that Wilde did not care for music—and still less for opera—means he may have been more critically aware of the comic possibilities of most opera *libretti;* and it is this outrageous manipulation of plot which enables [literary critic] Eric Bentley to declare that he has 'no serious plot, no credible characters', although it must be stressed that his characters are as credible within their dramatic context as are any in opera. . . . There is a greater truth than accuracy of character-drawing, and that is truth to the whole—in opera this is the music, and in Wilde's plays it is the verbal comedy.

The Construction of the Play

The construction of the play also rests on a series of secrets. It has sometimes been remarked that Wilde's plays (his social comedies, at any rate) depend on secrets: but it would be nearer the truth to say that the action arises from disclosure or the fear of disclosure. Deception and deceit are, in any case, the basis of most comedy; and *The Importance of Being Earnest* is no exception. Algernon goes down into the country under the pretext of visiting an invalid friend called Bunbury, while John Worthing J.P., excuses his absences from his country home by claiming to have a profligate brother called Ernest who lives at B.4, The Albany, then a somewhat raffish place of residence and eminently suitable for a disreputable bachelor whose immigration to Australia is under consideration. While in town John Worthing (who prefers to call himself Jack) is known as Ernest. In the first act he tells Gwendolen that he is staying in town until Monday but retreats to the country the very next day, presumably to announce the death of his fictitious brother Ernest and also to have himself christened under that name. After having obtained Jack's country address on the pretext that she might have to communicate with him urgently and after having made sure that he is remaining in London. Gwendolen goes down into the country the very next day to investigate his home background. After having overheard the conversation between Jack and Gwendolen, Algernon notes down this address and, pretending to be the profligate brother Ernest, manages to slither (accompanied by three portmanteaus, a dressing case, two hat-boxes, and a large luncheon-basket) into the country home and meet Cecily. Lady Bracknell is no less guileful in this respect: by bribing Gwendolen's maid she manages to find out where she has vanished; and her own life has been touched by scandal and mystery (and coincidences are not supposed to happen in the best families) when her infant nephew disappeared, together with his nursemaid, and could not be recovered despite the elaborate investigations of the metropolitan police who succeeded only in finding the perambulator standing by itself in a remote corner of Bayswater. Miss Prism has lived with the guilty secret of her misdeed (and without her invaluable hand-bag) for nearly thirty years. But John Worthing, J.P., *alias* Jack Worthing *alias* Ernest Worthing, has lived with even greater scandals: those of his unknown parents, of his having been *found*—and of his having been found in the cloak-room of one of the larger London railway stations, places known before now to have concealed social indiscretions. In the four act version there is an even greater scandal, when Algernon masquerading as Ernest Worthing is served with the writ for his unpaid account at the instigation of the Savoy Hotel, which seems to indicate that not only does John give himself up to a life of pleasure as Ernest but acts the part so fully as to run up debts in that name, a somewhat unnecessary course of action in view of his immense wealth. This wealth is also mysterious, for we learn little of the late Mr. Thomas Cardew, grandfather to Cecily and benefactor to John and who has left him a country house with about fifteen hundred acres attached to it, a town house at 149 Belgrave Square, and an income of between seven and eight thousand pounds a year. His lack of direct heirs is not referred to. It would have been interesting to know whether Mr. Cardew actually rose from the ranks of the aristocracy or was born in the purple of commerce: whatever the case he was in the exclusive Court Guides of the period and must have been among the wealthiest men in London. When John finds that the handbag in which he was found had belonged to Miss Prism he falls at her feet and calls her mother, willingly accepting that she was his unmarried mother. Of course, this is a piece of comic lunacy on Wilde's part—and to accept the fact that John is a bastard is a trifling matter after the various upheavals he has gone through. Nor is little Cecily above deceit, albeit of a petty kind, as when she tells Gwendolen that her engagement is to be announced in the local newspaper. The lives of the servants are no more impeccable: Lane, the manservant, was married in consequence of a misunderstanding between himself and a young person, a situation of which he speaks distantly. The entanglements of the plot proceed directly from Algernon's reading the inscription inside John's cigarette case—a clear parallel with the letters of *A Woman of No Importance* and *An*

Ideal Husband and the fan (another useless object of luxury) of *Lady Windermere's Fan*—which he has been holding on to since John last dined at home with him. Another instance of near-kleptodramatics! Deception and misunderstandings are the essence of farce and, to a lesser extent, of comedy, so that it is wrong to regard those in *The Importance of Being Earnest* in too serious a light. But their existence as part of the dramatic situation must be noted by the conscientious reader and stressed by both actors and producers. Though they are decidedly comic they might very well have been tragic; and there is nothing funny about an arrest of any kind, as Wilde was to learn for himself only a few weeks after the first performance of the play.

'Today', writes [English actor, producer, and drama critic] Sir John Gielgud, 'we laugh at the very idea that such types could ever have existed . . .' and goes on to mention 'the ridiculously exaggerated values of birth, rank and fashion'. He sees a danger that contemporary actors will turn the comedy into wild caricature because they lack 'real types to draw from'. At the same time, he writes of 'the grave puppet characters . . .' who 'utter their delicate cadences and spin their web of preposterously elegant sophistication'. Sir John is an experienced producer of the play and as John Worthing gave a superlative performance which older critics considered superior to that of [English director and actor George] Alexander, and his views are, therefore, of importance. But surely he is mistaken in his general attitude, for the play deals with lasting verities and with attitudes which are still prevalent in English life.

THE THEME OF LOVE AND MARRIAGE

In a manner not dissimilar from Shakespeare's comedies, *The Importance of Being Earnest* is concerned with young people, love and marriage; and as Shakespeare's comedies are generally set in the open air so Wilde sets his play in an English garden—in his first version three of the four acts were set there. At the end we are presented with declarations of love (which, it is to be presumed, imply proposals of marriage) by the two young couples as well as the older, graver Miss Prism and Canon Chasuble. The two young men are also, in a sense, regenerated by killing off their old Adams and seeking baptism—though not by total immersion. John soon declares his intention of killing off his brother and, in fact, announces that Ernest is 'Dead! . . . Quite dead', while Algernon kills off his *alter ego* Bunbury, 'Bunbury is dead . . . I killed Bunbury this afternoon . . . he was quite exploded.' If we take the intention of the two young men to be baptised as, in any sense, however comic, symbolic of their turning their backs on their old life and facing their new (married) life in an appropriate state of earnestness, we are reminded by Wilde that they are, in the Christian faith, already redeemed. The laughter arises not only from their casual attitude to christening but also from the different attitudes of Lady Bracknell and Canon Chasuble. Lady Bracknell does not underestimate the importance of christening, least of all in the financial sense, for she says that at John's birth he experienced it together with 'every luxury that money could buy', and his desire to be christened is described as 'grotesque and irreligious' and as an 'excess'—which, theologically speaking, it is. Canon Chasuble reinforces the theological attitudes when addressing Algernon, 'Yes, but you have been christened. That is the important thing.'

THE ROLE OF MONEY AND FOOD IN THE PLAY

The Importance of Being Earnest is earnest in quite a different way in its attitudes to two very material substances, both, at times, interchangeable: money and food. Eating and drinking whether of champagne or tea, cucumber sandwiches and bread-and-butter, cake, tea-cake, muffins or crumpets, whether in Algernon's flat, at Willis's or in the country, is a near-continuous activity which ferociously engages the characters' attention and passions. Algernon tells us, 'When I am in really great trouble, as anyone who knows me intimately will tell you, I refuse everything except food and drink.' The emotional scenes are those involving food, which is used as a weapon of warfare both personal and social. Thus cake is not eaten in the best houses any more (social aggrandisement); and, against her wishes Gwendolen is given cake and sugar is put in her tea (personal aggrandisement). The acquisitive instinct is aroused even more keenly by money, and Cecily's hundred and thirty thousand pounds—in the Funds. Lady Bracknell, indeed, rhapsodises on the subject: a large accumulation of property is eminently desirable even if the owner's youthful charms fade away during the process, for against human frailty is contrasted money, a real, solid quality, one of 'the qualities that last and improve with time'. As someone who before her marriage 'had no fortune of any kind' Lady Bracknell is clearly in a position to appreciate its value in others, as does her nephew Algernon who has nothing but his debts to rely on. The original four-act version, it should be remarked, had an act devoted to Algernon being arrested for the imaginary Ernest's debts.

Eric Bentley has pointed out that the very first scene between Algernon and his butler Lane is 'a prelude to the jokes against class society which run through the play'. Wilde, it is true, lets us see that Lane is not entirely defenceless; he establishes his right to help himself to the champagne in the blandest yet most defiant of fashions. Miss Prism reminds Cecily that watering the plants is a utilitarian (and, therefore, to be despised) occupation which belongs properly to the gardener. And Lady Bracknell believes that universal education is likely to result in 'acts of violence in Grosvenor Square'. The dialogue between Cecily and Gwendolen in the second act abounds with references to class, not the least being Gwendolen's assertion that she is happy to say she has never seen a spade. But so kind is Wilde's humour and his affection for these ruthless, acquisitive, snobbish characters all fighting for self-expression that he is content to establish the basic structure, the basic tone, and let the play speak for itself.

The Play's World of Linguistic Pleasure

Julia Prewitt Brown

Julia Prewitt Brown suggests that Wilde created a world onstage where the characters are earnestly and wholly committed to language and pleasure. Unlike the typical Victorian novel of Wilde's time, in which social determinism dictates the action, the dandies in *The Importance of Being Earnest* can repair the past and change their courses. It is, after all, a world in which the fictitious Ernest can become real. Brown maintains that the play is a linguistic world elevating language over character. Although the major characters have rudimentary desires, such as the intention to marry, they are primarily just a collection of words and witticisms.

Brown argues that Wilde held the notion that the people of his time were better geared to bear pain than they were to accept pleasure; hence, the playwright felt, one must learn to "suffer" pleasure. In *The Importance of Being Earnest,* people do not suffer and no one makes sacrifices.

Julia Prewitt Brown is a professor of English at Boston University in Massachusetts. She is the author of *Jane Austen's Novels: Social Change and Literary Form.*

In the cast of dandies of *The Importance of Being Earnest,* . . . no one suffers and no one sacrifices. The nursery-room atmosphere of *The Importance of Being Earnest,* in which the worst sin is the eating of muffins and its biggest threat the arrival of the nanny, Lady Bracknell, takes us into the world of later Victorian nonsense of [English writer of nonsense verse] Edward Lear and [English author] Lewis Carroll, as critics of the play have noted. In more recent years [English comedy group] *Monty Python* has recourse to Wilde's comic ideas, especially the idea of "going too far." Like the business-men in *Monty Python* who become carried away by "putting one thing on top of another," all of the characters in *The Importance of Being Earnest* go too far, like children acting up in the nursery, even to the point of performing their own bap-tism. The characters' notion of the rituals of life—of birth, baptism, and marriage—is entirely childlike and literal-minded, preoccupied only with form, with neatly arranging the surface of the gameboard so that the play can continue.

The plot of *The Importance of Being Earnest*, as Wilde knew, reflects the national myth of the century: the story of a person who was orphaned and who therefore is unsure of his name or identity, who eventually learns his true parent-age and name and who can therefore have a new beginning, as in a baptism, and marry. Whereas in the earlier plays, the pieties lodged in this myth are overturned by epigrams alone, both epigrams and action perform this function in *The Importance of Being Earnest.*

The central piety here is that of social determinism, the idea that we are built up by the influence of the environment and that our past determines the course of our lives. We are who we are as a result of the unchangeable covenants made early in life, like Pip's covenant with the criminal, Magwitch, in *Great Expectations* [novel by Charles Dickens]. But in *The Importance of Being Earnest* everything, the past above all, can be repaired. Algernon and Jack even go back to their own christenings. Ernest, a character who never existed, dies and is brought back to life, and no one bats an eye. The arrival of the supposedly dead Ernest mirrors every charac-ter in Victorian fiction who, like Raggles [character in William Thackeray's *Vanity Fair*] or Magwitch, returns to haunt the present and to confront the main character with the question of who he is: who is the real Ernest? But being Ernest and being earnest can never coincide because of the relative insincerity required of us to live in society. When the two are brought together, the play ends.

WILDE'S LINGUISTIC WORLD

In *Lady Windermere's Fan*, Victorian morality was reduced to a trivial object, a fan, which is an object of conspicuous consumption, a screen, and a beautiful thing. "The artist is the creator of beautiful things," wrote Wilde in the Preface to

The Picture of Dorian Gray. In the dandyish aestheticism of *Lady Windermere's Fan,* language and art are screens. In *A Woman of No Importance,* which concerns itself with the unmasking of stereotypes, the "reality" beneath them is exposed. But in *The Importance of Being Earnest,* the surface of language is presented to us as the only reality and the play *appears* to be celebrating the self-sufficiency of language in itself. It could be argued that the characters are mere assemblages of words or witticisms and that the language of the epoch speaks them, not the reverse. For at the same time that nothing is determined in the play's action—so different from the deployment of action in the Victorian novel—everything here is determined by language. Cecily is engaged to be married to Algernon three months before they meet: "You can see the entry if you like," she assures him, pointing to her diary.

In this vibrating linguistic universe, "The only really safe name is Ernest," says a character, wisely concerned with safety. In order to participate in the society or its institutions, such as marriage, some claim to a consistent identity must be made so that we may recognize one another, literally by *name.* Knowing this (in a play in which all of the characters are so innocently knowing), Jack and Algernon seek to establish themselves in the hearts and minds of the women characters by means of baptism, the naming ritual. It would seem that in the world of play "there is no event or thing . . . that does not in some way partake of language. . . . We cannot imagine a total absence of language in anything." Wilde playfully anticipates [German essayist Walter] Benjamin's philosophy of language (in "The Critic as Artist" he had written that language is "the parent, and not the child of thought"), although keeping it within a predictable set of 'realistic' human concerns.

Not that *The Importance of Being Earnest* is without magic. A character who never existed is brought back to life when someone claims his name; characters come up with pasts for one another by pointing to a diary, register, and handbag. But all of this is understood by an audience whose response takes the form of rational amusement, not simply over the supposed ubiquitousness of language, but over the characters' earnest relation to it. In order for the play to amuse, the absolute earnestness of the characters' prattle must be taken for granted. For although each character is an assemblage of words, each possesses an *intention*: the intention to marry. Wilde returns playfully to the biological origins of the comic genre in this most cerebral of plays. In the Anthony Asquith film version of the play, for example, Michael Redgrave plays Jack as someone wholly earnest and in love, who can barely hold a teacup without dropping it when in the presence of his beloved. Irony, wit, cynicism are qualities strangely external to the characters in this performance, who are wholly unconscious of what they are saying. When Cecily is about to meet the man she thinks is her scapegrace cousin, she says: "I have never met any really wicked person before. I feel rather frightened. I am so afraid he will look just like everyone else." And after she meets him she says indignantly: "I hope you have not been leading a double life, pretending to be wicked and being really good all the time. That would be hypocrisy." The humor is not simply in what she is saying but in her absolute earnestness toward the man with whom she has already fallen in love. Our emotions, as an audience, are thus engaged not by our sense of the characters' innocence but by their charm. By conventional standards, they are all, every one of them, corrupt. But Wilde's aim is to suggest that not all *standards* are serious.

WILDE'S WORLD OF PLEASURE

The only thing that could date *The Importance of Being Earnest*, then, would be if directors ceased to take the characters seriously and misdirected the actors to perform with knowing wit and cynicism. This happens from time to time in revivals that fail because of their insipidity. The humor of the play depends upon the characters' absolutely terrifying dependence on the power of language and naming. As in [film actor and director] Charlie Chaplin's performances, we must fear for the comic figure in order to be amused by him, and to fear for him we must trust his intentions. The tension in this sort of comedy, which resembles that accompanying the acrobatic paradoxes of "The Decay of Lying," is something that we must bear, as we watch, for example, Chaplin rollerskate on the edge of a precipice. In the *Laws*, Plato said that we must learn to bear pleasure as well as pain, and those who dislike *The Importance of Being Earnest* (like [Irish playwright] George Bernard Shaw and [literary critic] Mary McCarthy, who found it to be cold-hearted) are perhaps unprepared to do this. It was Wilde's contention that in his century people as a rule were far more prepared to bear pain than pleasure, and found the former far easier to do. Each generation has its revival of *The Importance of Being Earnest* to remind us of this task. Because of its perpetual challenge, the play is still ahead of its time. Wilde knew he was playing with fire when he wrote it: "How I used to toy with that tiger Life!" he wrote to Reginald Turner, possibly alluding to the homosexual subtext of the action: the secret life of "bunburying." Having passed through the purifying fires of the earlier plays in which a Christian aesthetic of pain is exorcised, Wilde, who literally had to bear his pleasures, understood that pleasure is as realizable as pain. To bear pleasure—that is, to suffer it as well as to give it birth—is what the play is about, a burden that has everything to do with language. For Algernon and Jack do not move forward in time toward death, but backward in time toward their own christening, to the paradisiac moment of naming. After this creative moment, after the fall into language, all else becomes empty "prattle," in the profound sense in which [Danish philosopher Søren] Kierkegaard uses the word. That *The Importance of Being Earnest* is composed of such prattle is what disturbed Mary McCarthy, who compared it to the suffocating world of [French philosopher and writer] Jean-Paul

Sartre's *No Exit.* Yet within that idle world of prattle Alger-non and Jack work surprisingly hard toward freeing them-selves of it by returning to the original word, which, ironi-cally enough, is *earnest* (or Ernest).

The abrupt conclusion of the action, in which the pun on "being Ernest" is loudly proclaimed and the play seems to disappear into the sky like a balloon whose string has been cut, intensifies our feeling that the play's language is a labyrinth in which the characters are forever doomed to wander and play, utterly separate from the circumstantial world in which we ourselves live. This lightness is an es-sential element in Wilde's theory of art in general; and, as [literary critic Theodor] Adorno suggests, it holds for art as a whole, even works preoccupied with the horrors of reality: "Even in [French dramatist Samuel] Beckett's plays the cur-tain rises the way it rises on the room with the Christmas presents." But *The Importance of Being Earnest* is unique— "a genre in itself," as critics have recognized—in its delight in the fact of its own existence, that it is art at all. It was in the period of its composition that Wilde's utopianism in fact peaked. On holiday in Algiers shortly before the first trial, he had remarked to [French writer André] Gide, "The sun is jealous of art."

Wilde as a Master Epigrammist

Francesca Coppa

Francesca Coppa credits Oscar Wilde as a master epigrammist: He used word structures to cite or rework established knowledge. When audience members understand an epigram, they derive pleasure from being in on the joke and share the authority of the epigrammist. Hence, an epigrammatic play like *The Importance of Being Earnest* creates an elitist group, those who get it based on an understanding of the knowledge restructured by the epigrammist.

According to Coppa, Wilde revamps a vast knowledge of theatrical knowledge in *The Importance of Being Earnest*. He cuts, cites, and alters details from a wide array of Victorian plays, reinventing them within established theatrical discourses. As an epigrammatic playwright, Wilde remakes what the audience already knows.

Francesca Coppa wrote the following essay as a graduate student in the Victorian Studies Group at Fales Library, New York University.

Oscar Wilde's primary literary genius was as an epigrammist. By this I do not mean that Wilde's wit outweighs his work; rather, I am suggesting that understanding the full impact of Wilde's theatrical output means fully coming to grips with the literary form of which he remains the undisputed master. All of Wilde's works have epigrams liberally sprinkled throughout them; however, his works are related to the epigram in more significant ways than this. Wilde's plays are structured like epigrams, have the same concerns, are formed by the same processes, were written by the same writer. A man who writes epigrams, writes epigrams, and one can find the epigram in Wilde's work not only with a microscope, but with a telescope.

Excerpted from " 'I seem to recognize a device that has done duty in bygone plays': Oscar Wilde and the Theatre of Epigram," by Francesca Coppa in *Reading Wilde: Querying Spaces* (New York: Fales Library, 1995). Reprinted with permission from Fales Library and the author.

An epigrammist is, above all, a master of discourses. Epigrams are a knowledge game, a demonstration of their author's mastery. In Wilde's time, this game was a common and popular one, attested to by collections of famous writers' bon mots, printed in handy pocket editions: a literary tradition copied from eighteenth-century wits. However, after Wilde's downfall, the epigram also fell into intellectual disrepute. In the introduction to a 1945 collection of epigrams, *World's Wit and Wisdom* editor [literary critic and editor] Norman Lockridge is quick to assert that epigrams have "no creative importance." He supports this statement by claiming that the thoughts of epigrams "seem to derive from *words* instead of actual *things*." But epigrams do refer to "actual things"—but those actual things are words, genres, texts, ideas, and previous formulations of knowledge. In the years since Lockridge wrote his dismissive introduction, literary criticism has come to think that "creative importance" stems more from mastery of the frisson between words than from the representation of reality, which is to say that literary criticism has come to realize the importance of Wilde's position, if not specifically of the epigrammatic genre within which he wrote.

RESTRUCTURED KNOWLEDGE IN AN EPIGRAM

Epigrams have several distinctive features. Centrally, as I have said, they illustrate their author's mastery of discourses. This occurs in several ways. Epigrams are always citing and negotiating with one or more previous formulations of knowledge. This distinguishes them from proverbs or maxims, which they are otherwise structured to resemble. Proverbs and maxims tend to be a first literary formulation of an idea; epigrams, in contrast, intervene only in already-established formations. Only after an idea has been publicly articulated can an epigram upon it be written. As Wilde put it, "I appropriate what is already mine, for once a thing is published it becomes public property." On this premise, John Heywood, dramatist and epigrammist of the sixteenth century, was able to write within the genre of "epigrams upon proverbs":

> *Better one bird in hand, than ten in the wood:*
> *Better for birders, but for birds not so good.*

Heywood is not just building on the "public property" of proverbs; he is intervening in the public ideology that constructs them, articulating a position against the "they" of "as they say. . . ." Similarly, when Oscar Wilde, 330 years after Heywood, notes that, "History never repeats itself. The historians repeat each other," he is speaking as a critic of the [still] common wisdom that informs popular discourse about history.

One of the results of this process of citation and negotiation is that the epigram derives authority from the audience's familiarity with the proverbial ideas upon which it is built. The form of the epigram is always short and memorable, and its incorporation and alteration of already-familiar ideas renders it all the more powerful. The interventionist position of the epigram gives the author all the powers of both a creator and a critic: one appreciates the originality with which the epigram writer is able to recreate an already mapped-out intellectual territory. And the epigram always does *re*-create the world by taking as its subject already-marked areas of intellectual thought; in fact, an epigram writer *defines* the world as the sum total of all the competing discourses about it. Not just the epigram, but the world is defined by words and not by "actual things." History doesn't repeat itself; historians repeat themselves. History is what historians repeat.

THE IMPERSONAL QUALITY OF AN EPIGRAM

Like historians, who gain power through repetition, epigrammists, too, gain additional authority by being repeated. Wilde, one of the most quoted writers in history, established this pattern by frequently quoting himself; his best lines tend to appear in more than one of his works. Wilde's re-use of his own epigrams illustrates another of the form's unusual qualities—its impersonality. This may seem a strange attribute of a genre so concerned with exhibiting the mastery of its author. After all, the epigrammatic language Wilde used was—and still is—identified with him personally. [American novelist] Henry James, for example, after seeing *Lady Windermere's Fan,* remarked in a letter that "There is of course absolutely no characterization and all the people talk equally strained Oscar." Wilde's characters speak a language so highly identified with its author that the implicit criticism is that all the characters are simply Wilde himself in different guises. However, epigrams are structured in such a way that it is possible for them to come from the mouths of many different characters—they are not tied to a specific individual, not even Oscar Wilde. Compare this to the humor of a [American film director, actor, and writer] Woody Allen, whose most amusing lines must, necessarily, be said by Woody Allen, as they usually refer to the specific personality quirks of Woody Allen. Instead, the epigrammatic personality becomes that of any authoritative speaker, aligning the epigrammist with all other masters and authorities. The epigram therefore becomes a perfect symbol for Wilde's artistic game: the genre within which he worked simultaneously asserts and effaces the personality, asserts individuality and yet hides behind the authority of already-familiar modes of expression.

Wilde's plays, which contain so many of his epigrams, function as epigrams themselves, and illustrate Wilde's complete authority over the theatrical discourses of his day. For example, in a review of *The Importance of Being Earnest* dated February 23, 1895, the reviewer notes that:

> *The most successful situation in the farce is the appearance of Mr Alexander [playing Jack] in deep mourning for the loss of an imaginary brother . . . in the course of an adventure described as "Bunburying." Bunbury is a mythical friend who has a habit of summoning Mr. Aynesworth [playing Algernon] to his sick bed when that young man finds it convenient to disappear. I seem to recognize in Bunbury a device that has done duty in bygone plays. In "Pink Dominoes," for instance, it was the state of the cotton market at Manchester that compelled a flighty gentleman to make a pretense of leaving town . . . But if Mr. Wilde has not invented an absolutely new deception for farce, his Bunbury is a delightful notion for all that.*

"Absolutely new" is hardly the point. The reviewer has perceptively noted that Bunburying is a device "that has done duty in bygone plays," but what he has not noticed is Wilde's naming, and in this case it is a "proper" naming—or, even more accurately—a proper *re*-naming, of that device. Many other plays have used it, consciously or unconsciously. Authors sometimes find it necessary to remove characters from a situation: characters sometimes find the need to remove themselves. It's an all-too-common dramatic action: the doorbell rings, a character suddenly declares that he must check the state of the cotton market in Manchester. Now, however, it is Bunburying: by overtly articulating the situation, by claiming it, Wilde has named it, he owns it. The "common" theatrical gesture has been remapped; the proverbial has been cited and claimed.

What the reviewer has also failed to notice is his own pleasure of recognition. Wilde has allowed him to show himself for the expert he no doubt is: he can say that he recognizes the Bunbury device, he gets to illustrate his theatrical breadth by citing *Pink Dominoes.* This is another result of epigrammatic writing: those who understand what discourse is being played with get to share the position of authority with the epigrammist. This is necessary for the epigrammist's illustration of his mastery: someone with the necessary knowledge must notice and appreciate what he has done. Wilde's friend, the actress Elizabeth Robins, was observing this dynamic when she noted that, "Oscar Wilde was born more a creature of the theatre than most actors are. He needed the audience. He could not do his best without the audience." Henry James was more specific in describing the role of the audience in Wilde's plays.

> There is so much drollery—that is, 'cheeky" or paradoxical wit or dialogue, and the pit and gallery are so pleased at finding themselves clever enough to "catch on" to four or five of the ingenious—too ingenious—mots in the dozen, that it makes them feel quite "décadent" and "raffiné" and they enjoy the sensation as a change from the stodgy.

James notices the pleasure Wilde's audience gets from being "in" on the epigrammatic jokes, though he seems to resent Wilde's sharing his discursive mastery with mere members of the pit and gallery. Wilde is establishing an alternate aristocracy of the "ins" and "outs," with knowledge, not money or birth, required for membership. Wilde thus shares the pleasure of being in an elitist community with his audience, and no doubt enjoys being thought clever by every socioeconomic level. And James fails to identify his own critical stance toward Wilde as just another example of the human desire to feel "décadent" and "raffiné": it's lovely to feel clever enough to deconstruct someone else's too-ingenious work.

THE IMPORTANCE OF BEING EARNEST AS AN EPIGRAM

If the pit and gallery "caught on" to some of the epigrams, and the critics "caught on" to some of the larger epigrammatic issues in the plays, it takes a scholarly fervor to analyze all of the epigrammatic gestures in *The Importance of Being Earnest.* In his book, *Oscar Wilde and The Theatre of the 1890s,* [literary critic] Kerry Powell points out that while *The Importance of Being Earnest* is generally thought to be Oscar Wilde's most original work, it is actually the play which has "stolen" most from other plays of the day. It is, of course, both: because Wilde is an epigrammatic writer, his "most original" play would be one which illustrates his complete theatrical mastery, the play that allows for the largest re-mapping of theatrical territory. Powell points out that a play called *The Foundling* (by W. Lestocq), in which "a young man's comic difficulties in romance are caused by having 'lost' his parents" provided the base plot for *Earnest*. The rest of Wilde's "original" details come from his citing and altering the details of a large number of Victorian plays. Powell writes:

> *Algernon Moncrieff's gluttonizing of muffins and cucumber sandwiches in Wilde's play is reminiscent generally of the ritual food gags of Victorian farce—from pouring tea in a hat in Charley's Aunt to throwing bacon and chops out the window in Box and Cox. . . . Labiche and Delacour's Celimare le bien aimé anticipates the "Bunburying" motif in* Earnest *by presenting an imaginary invalid whose feigned illness is used to escape certain social responsibilities. In Musset's* Il ne faut jurer de rien . . . *an ingenue named Cécile—rather than Cecily, as in Wilde's play—is the reluctant pupil of her clerical tutor and falls in love with a young man pretending to be someone else. In W.S. Gilbert's* Engaged *two young women turn from gushing friendship to hostility when they discover one may have inadvertently married the other's fiancé, anticipating a similar development between Cecily Cardew and Gwendolen Moncrieff in* Earnest. *And like Jack Worthing in Wilde's play, one of the characters in* Engaged *comes to stage dressed in deep mourning for what turns out to be only an imaginary death. But this device had already been used by John Maddison Morton, whose* A Husband to Order *has a character enter "in a black costume," disguised as his own brother, mourning his own make-believe death.*

Powell details a number of Wilde's forgotten sources, with the aim of providing a view of the mostly unpreserved Victorian theatre scene and Wilde's intimacy with it. However, at the end he concludes that because there are so many influences in Wilde's work, for all practical purposes there are none. Wilde's work, despite all this intertextuality, is not derivative. The relationship between Wilde and his sources makes sense only when one realizes that this process of play writing mirrors the process of epigrammatizing. Wilde is not stealing any particular notion, but a proverbial notion. His plays are epigrams, intervening in already established theatrical discourses. . . .

This epigrammatic is not only Wilde's process, but also his subject. Wilde reclaims the woman with a past, Wilde re-

WILDE'S SELF-ASSESSMENT

Between January and March 1897, Wilde, while still in prison, wrote a famous letter in which he reflects on his role as a writer.

The gods had given me almost everything. I had genius, a distinguished name, high social position, brilliancy, intellectual daring: I made art a philosophy, and philosophy an art: I altered the minds of men and the colours of things: there was nothing I said or did that did not make people wonder: I took the drama, the most objective form known to art, and made it as personal a mode of expression as the lyric or the sonnet, at the same time that I widened its range and enriched its characterisation: drama, novel, poem in rhyme, poem in prose, subtle or fantastic dialogue, whatever I touched I made beautiful in a new mode of beauty: to truth itself I gave what is false no less than what is true as its rightful province, and showed that the false and the true are merely forms of intellectual existence. I treated Art as the supreme reality, and life as a mere mode of fiction: I awoke the imagination of my century so that it created myth and legend around me: I summed up all systems in a phrase, and all existence in an epigram.

Oscar Wilde, in Anne Varty, *A Preface to Oscar Wilde*. London: Longman, 1988, p. 211.

names Bunbury, Wilde reverses [English dramatist and actor Sir Arthur Wing] Pinero. But his plays are also about the process of citing, claiming, and renaming. In the introduction to his biography of Wilde, Richard Ellmann claims that "while the ultimate virtue in Wilde's essays is in make-believe, the denouement of his drama and narratives is that masks have to go. We must acknowledge who we are." But, Wilde himself has told us that it is art that makes us what we are: life imitates art, nature imitates art. So perhaps we need to acknowledge what art makes of us. And the artist, Wilde claims, never invents. He cites. He negotiates. "The true artist is known by the use he makes of what he annexes, and he annexes everything." All of which is an elaborate way of saying that the self is the ultimate work of art, and like a work of art, like the world, it is the sum total of all the discourses about it. Like a chameleon, the self can only be seen in relation to a background, and can only be known by what use it makes of these recognizable background discourses. If we don't make conscious, unique, *artistic* use of the discourses around us, we are all merely abstract concepts, theatrical tropes of one kind or another. If we don't master the discourses, the discourses will master us.

Wilde's characters speak in epigram, but their identities are also epigrammatic. Wilde does not tell stories about their unmasking, but about their negotiations for a personal place in the already mapped out space of character and personality (a space as highly marked outside the theatre as within it). Ironically, Wilde himself lost his ability to negotiate his own identity during his trials, which were consciously targeted at exploding his epigrammatic ability. During the course of his cross-examination, Wilde was repeatedly asked to *explain* his various epigrams. Having to explain negates the entire epigrammatic position: the discourses are suddenly claimed unfamiliar, the intervention unrecognizable, the mastery invalid, and the epigram unrepeatable. The epigrammist is silenced. But each time we see one of Wilde's plays, we get to see successful epigrammatology at work. Through that process, the characters achieve the new, the original, the epigrammatic. Night after night, the theatre's Jack is claimed and becomes Wilde's Ernest.

Wilde's Painstaking Writing Process

Russell Jackson

Russell Jackson debunks the impression Wilde liked to give that his works flowed effortlessly from his pen, emanating more from inspiration than hard work. In reality, Wilde was a meticulous craftsman who tirelessly reworked his art, making countless adjustments and attending to the most trivial details. Wilde was also a master of public relations: Jackson explains that the playwright's quick wit and ability to provide entertaining epigrammatic utterances made him extremely popular with journalists.

Jackson argues that *The Importance of Being Earnest* is different from Wilde's earlier work due to several omissions and deviations. Jackson explains that many of the stock characters that the audience might expect are missing. For example, the play does not include a "woman with a past" character or an innocent, idealistic young woman who must face the harshness of society. Unlike previous male characters, the men are cultivated but not villainous or nonchalantly virtuous.

Russell Jackson is deputy director of the Shakespeare Institute at the University of Birmingham in Stratford-upon-Avon. He is the author of *Victorian Theatre: A New Mermaid Sourcebook.*

The Importance of Being Earnest, Oscar Wilde's most famous and—posthumously—most successful play, was first produced by George Alexander at the St James's Theatre on 14 February 1895. London was enduring a prolonged and severe spell of cold weather: several theatres advertised their steam-heating among the attractions of their programme, and the first night of Wilde's comedy had been put off from

12 February because several of the women in the cast had bad colds. In addition to the habitual glamour of a first night at a fashionable theatre, the occasion was especially interesting because Wilde was in vogue. *An Ideal Husband* had been playing at the Haymarket Theatre since 3 January, and at the same theatre *A Woman of No Importance* had completed a successful run, having opened on 19 April 1893. On 20 February 1892. *Lady Windermere's Fan* had been the second play staged by Alexander's new management at the St James's Theatre, running until 26 July of that year.

Wilde's spectacular début in the early 1880s had been followed by a period of less glamorous work as a reviewer, editor and jobbing author for journals and magazines. In 1888 he published *The Happy Prince and Other Tales.* In 1891 he had published four books, including *The Picture of Dorian Gray* and *Intentions.* Now, a decade after his appearance on the London literary scene, he was a successful West End dramatist and was beginning to seem a more substantial figure. A book-length lampoon, *The Green Carnation,* by imitating (perhaps reporting) his style of conversation, contributed to his renewed prominence in the literary and social gossip columns. To some readers it may also have suggested—or confirmed—the impression that there was a less positive side to Wilde's notoriety.

For his part, George Alexander was a rising theatrical star. He had gone into management in 1889 after establishing himself during a stint with Henry Irving's company at the Lyceum. In 1891 he had taken the St James's Theatre, where he remained until his death in 1915. He was knighted in 1911. Alexander's theatre was run meticulously. His biographer, the playwright and novelist A.E.W. Mason, described Alexander's work on one of his own plays. The manager went through the script line by line and move by move, interrogating him rigorously on every sentence, and planning moves with a toy theatre stage. Then a ground cloth was marked with the lines of walls and exits and for three weeks there were daily rehearsals, beginning each day punctually at eleven and finishing at two, until for the last four days there were morning and afternoon sessions, culminating in two dress-rehearsals. The management's attention to detail in staging and performance was thorough: Lady Alexander described how on a first night she would sit in her box 'sick with anxiety' and then between the acts 'I used to put on an apron and go behind the scenes to place all the little things on the stage myself until the men got used to it. I arranged the flowers; in those days we had so much detail, and I loved to make things look real. I ordered the gowns to suit the decorations of the scene so that nothing clashed or was ugly. Alec gave me the large sum of £5 a week for my work, and I think I was very cheap at the price. . . .

WILDE'S METICULOUS REWRITING

It might never have appeared so in public, but Wilde resembled Alexander in his approach to work. Their temperaments were dissimilar in other respects, but both were scrupulous, laborious artists. Wilde liked to give the impression that words flowed easily from his pen, but this was part of a strategy for undermining assumptions about the seriousness of art. In fact, his new 'Trivial Comedy for Serious People' (or, in earlier drafts, 'serious comedy for trivial people') was proposed in outline to George Alexander in July 1894, drafted in August and assiduously revised and polished during the autumn. Alexander had not taken it up at first, and Wilde placed it with Charles Wyndham, who had not so far staged any of his plays. In the event *The Importance of Being Earnest* came to the St James's when the failure of Henry James's *Guy Domville* made a replacement necessary. (Unable to face his own first night, James had tried to distract himself by going to see *An Ideal Husband* at the Haymarket.) In the course of rehearsal, among other adjustments to the text, Alexander insisted that the play be reduced from four to three acts. This is the best-known and most radical alteration made between the first draft and the first night, but Wilde had revised every sequence, most speeches and almost every sentence over the past six months.

Some of the changes might seem trivial in themselves, but in a play so economical in its language and effects, they had a serious consequence. Thus, Wilde considered several variations of the title of Dr Chasuble's sermon, which was given for benefit of a charity described at one time or another as the Society for the Prevention of 'Cruelty to Children' (a real organisation, and therefore not really suitable), 'Discontent among the Higher Orders' and, in the page-proofs of the 1899 edition, 'Discontent among the Lower Orders'. Wilde finally altered this to 'Discontent among the Upper Orders', restoring a topsy-turvy joke of a kind familiar in the play.

Sometimes in an early manuscript draft one finds the bare bones of a speech later developed and made specific to its speaker and the situation. Thus Wilde produced the following:

> O! it is absurd to have a hard-and-fast rule about what one should read and one shouldn't. More than half of modern culture depends on what one shouldn't read.

from this (manuscript draft):

> One should read everything. That is the true basis of modern culture. More than half of modern culture depends on the unreadable.

In the first edition (1899) Jack declares to Gwendolen:

> Miss Fairfax, ever since I met you I have admired you more than any girl—I have ever met since—I met you.

The faltering is carefully indicated by Wilde with inserted dashes. The earliest draft of the speech makes it a self-consciously clever and confident sentence, with a play on words that depends on emphasis:

> Miss Fairfax, ever since I *met* you I have admired you more than any girl I have met since I met *you.*

Among the multitude of similar tinkerings is one which seems puzzling. When Lady Bracknell is told that Jack has lost both his parents, the earliest manuscript draft of the complete act has her react as follows:

> Both? . . . To lose one parent may be considered a misfortune. To lose both seems like carelessness.

It seems likely that in 1895 the line was spoken thus:

> Both? To lose one parent may be regarded as a misfortune, to lose both seems like carelessness.

This was the version of the line printed in the page-proofs for the first edition: Wilde changed it to

> Both?—that seems like carelessness.

As if this were not puzzling enough, Robert Ross, in the first collected edition of Wilde's works, printed yet another variation:

> Both? To lose one parent, Mr Worthing, may be regarded as a misfortune; to lose both looks like carelessness.

Wilde's alteration and Ross's emendation have yet to be explained.

WILDE'S TASTE FOR PUBLICITY

This fine tuning is part of a process that Wilde was careful to conceal beneath the image of an artist who worked by inspiration and *sprezzatura* [Italian word suggesting spontaneity and virtuosity], composing almost in spite of himself. He was a master of what would now be called media opportunities. His epigrammatic, paradoxical utterances made for effective publicity, *fin-de-siècle* sound-bites. The vigorous world of the expanding and increasingly illustrated popular press gave scope for interviews, paragraphs in gossip columns, glimpses of celebrities 'at home', cartoons, parodies, reports of speeches (especially first-night speeches) and lectures. Wilde made great play with the boundary between public and private personality, affecting a kind of lofty intimacy which tantalised journalists and their public. He was always good copy, never at a loss for words and frequently trod a narrow path between effrontery and reserve. In an interview with [journalist and Wilde's friend] Robert Ross, published on 18 January 1895, Wilde answers the tentative enquiry, 'I dare not ask, I suppose, whether [the play] will please the public?' with a splendidly definitive statement:

> When a play that is a work of art is produced on the stage, what is being tested is not the play, but the stage; when a play that is *not* a work of art is produced on the stage what is being tested is not the play, but the public.

Such a 'personality', effortlessly generating publicity, was in one sense a godsend to Alexander, but there was another side to Wilde's presentation of himself. It is clear from some reviews of the plays that Wilde was thought to have intruded himself, to be passing off 'false' wit as 'true' (by Victorian definitions). Some critics used the word 'impertinence' ominously and equivocally to describe both the style and the author. In February 1895 more than one critic wondered whether the fashion for Wilde's paradoxical, epigrammatic wit would survive. However pleasing *The Importance of Being Earnest* might be (and even the sourest reviewers could not ignore its success with audiences), would the new style continue to appeal to the public?

The Importance of Being Earnest has, of course, prevailed. It is one of the few plays from its period to remain in theatrical repertoires, outlasting most of the trivial and almost all the serious works of Wilde's contemporaries. W.S. Gilbert has barely survived without Sullivan's support, Arthur Wing Pinero's farces from the 1880s are far more commonly seen than the later work he set most store by, plays by Henry Arthur Jones have received only a few revivals, and such erstwhile celebrities as Haddon Chambers and Sydney

Grundy have sunk without trace. From the theatres of the nineties, only the plays of Wilde and [Irish dramatist George Bernard] Shaw have consistently held the stage, together with Brandon Thomas's farce *Charley's Aunt* (1892). Of Wilde's own plays, it is *The Importance of Being Earnest* which has enjoyed most revivals.

If Wilde were here now he might well express surprise at posterity's behaviour. As far as he was concerned, *The Importance of Being Earnest* was not the culmination, and of course not at all the conclusion, of a dramatic career. He was anxious to write a more serious play, also sketched in the summer of 1894, and when he first broached the subject of the new comedy to Alexander (asking for an advance of £150) he referred to it as his response to an American impresario's request for a play 'with no real serious interest'. This attitude to *The Importance of Being Earnest* persisted in his letters to Alexander during the autumn, Wilde declaring that it would probably be unsuitable for the more serious repertoire the manager was establishing for the St James's company and wished to take with him on a projected American tour. Wilde's Society plays before *The Importance of Being Earnest* can be seen as a series of experiments, determinedly distorting familiar dramatic situations. This new play seems an excursion—a day-trip into a less demanding, less adventurous kind of theatre. Certainly it appeared so to a number of reviewers, especially those who regarded the unevenness of the earlier plays as signs of Wilde's inadequate grasp of the essentials of construction and character. *The Importance of Being Earnest* lacks not only the 'serious' plot devices of the other Society plays, but also the grandiloquent speeches with which the characters rise to serious subjects in moments of crisis. When we approach *The Importance of Being Earnest* as his first audiences did, from experience of Wilde's previous West End plays and his perceived characteristics as a writer, it seems remarkable for a number of omissions and deviations from what might be expected.

WILDE'S SPLIT FROM DRAMATIC EXPECTATIONS

Three figures prominent in Wilde's previous dramatic work are absent. The new comedy lacks a 'woman with a past' like the active and defiant Mrs Erlynne [from *Lady Windermere's Fan*] or Mrs Cheveley [from *An Ideal Husband*], or the wronged and repentant Mrs Arbuthnot [from *A Woman of*

No Importance]. (Miss Prism does not emerge as a comic variation on this theme until the final scenes.) In fact, the past in this play has become a benign rather than a menacing secret, with the handbag concealing not a 'social indiscretion' but an absurd mistake. Female culpability (a mainspring even of the 'advanced' serious drama of the time) is limited to absent-mindedness. An audience in February 1895 might also have expected a dandyish aristocrat of Wilde's particular kind—either dubiously charming like Darlington in *Lady Windermere's Fan,* villainous like Illingworth in *A Woman of No Importance* or nonchalantly virtuous like Goring in *An Ideal Husband.* Both Algernon and Jack (in his London mode) lead lives of cultivated pointlessness, and both are given to making authoritative statements on all aspects of modern life and culture (so, for that matter are Gwendolen, Cecily and Lady Bracknell) but neither of the men is a villain or a *raisonneur.* Like the stories of the plays in which Wilde had so far used them, the woman with a past and the dandy were Wildean revisions of the stock devices, and a playgoer might expect that a new play by him would continue to exploit this vein. The third stock figure that *The Importance of Being Earnest* lacks is the innocently idealistic young woman, forced to confront the sordid realities of political and social life—Hester Worsley in *A Woman of No Importance,* or Lady Windermere and Lady Chiltern, all of them gifted with a kind of rhetoric that it is hard to believe the author took seriously. Again, the new play transforms a type, in this instance by making idealism consist in wanting to marry a man called Ernest, and self-righteous indignation is briefly mocked when the two girls declare that they have been deceived by Jack and Algernon.

Another quality associated with Wilde in the early 1890s is also notably absent: self-conscious 'decadence'. *Salomé* (published but refused a performance licence) combined oriental exoticism with perverse passions. *The Picture of Dorian Gray* had confirmed the association of his name with the luxuriant description of unusual and refined artistic tastes, and the theme of a younger man seduced intellectually and aesthetically (and perhaps implicitly, sexually) by an older mentor. In his critical dialogues, 'The Critic as Artist' and 'The Decay of Lying', aesthetic discrimination is associated with luxurious surroundings and the idea of persuasive talk among men. Persuasion and conviction are central to the fictional 'Portrait of Mr W.H.' One of the real dangers of *The Green Carnation*—given Wilde's personal situation in 1894—was its suggestion of such a relationship between the Wilde figure and a young man. In the first two West End plays there is relatively little of this element—at least on the surface, although Gerald Arbuthnot is clearly under the spell of the man who is revealed to be his father. In *An Ideal Husband* the theme is handled explicitly. Sir Robert Chiltern's wealth and career have been based on a dishonest act committed at the instance of a sinister international financier, Baron Arnheim. Chiltern describes Arnheim's influence in terms redolent of the corruption of Dorian Gray by Lord Henry Wotton:

> I remember so well how, with a strange smile on his pale, curved lips, he led me through his wonderful picture gallery, showed me his tapestries, his enamels, his jewels, his carved ivories, made me wonder at all the strange loveliness of the luxury in which he lived; and then told me that luxury was nothing but a background, a painted scene in a play, and that power, power over other men, power over the world, was the one thing worth having, the one supreme pleasure worth knowing, the joy one never tired of, and that in our century only the rich possessed it.

This overtly 'decadent' vein (toned down in the revision of *An Ideal Husband*) is entirely absent from the farce. As if to draw attention to the missing element, a contemporary parody in *Punch* by a friend of Wilde makes a joke of infusing the new play with decadence. Ada Leverson's 'The Advisability of Not Being Brought Up in a Hand-Bag' features 'Dorian', described in the cast-list as 'a button-hole':

> ALGY: (*eating cucumber-sandwiches*). Do you know, Aunt Augusta, I am afraid I shall not be able to come to your dinner to-night, after all. My friend Bunbury has had a relapse, and my place is by his side.
> AUNT AUGUSTA: (*drinking tea*). Really, Algy! it will put my table out dreadfully. And who will arrange my music?
> DORIAN: *I* will arrange your music, Aunt Augusta. I know all about music. I have an extraordinary collection of musical instruments. I give curious concerts every Wednesday in a long latticed room, where wild gipsies tear mad music from little zithers, and I have brown algerians who beat monotonously upon copper drums. Besides, I have set myself to music. And it has not marred me. I am still the same. More so, if anything.

Although it is arguable that there are coded references to the homosexual double life of its author in the play, nothing of the overtly Dorian mode is to be found in the finished work or its drafts. Algernon's rooms may be 'luxuriously and artistically furnished', but he never speaks anything remotely resembling the language of decadence. His debts are the conventional attribute of the stage man about town. The manuscript draft of the first act seems to suggest that Wilde thought of making the need for a fortune into a motivation for Algernon's pursuit of Jack's young ward—although this was not followed up and the hint was soon removed. (Interestingly, this would have made the play more like Gilbert's cynical comedy *Engaged,* with its principal characters avidly pursuing money while spouting the rhetoric of love.)

The opening scene of the four-act version has Algernon besieged in Half-Moon Street by creditors (represented eventually simply by the letters Lane hands him in the first scene), and in a sequence subsequently cut from the second act a solicitor pursues him to the country to arrest him for a debt of £762.14s.2d. for dinners at the Savoy Hotel. ('There can be little good in any young man who eats so much, and so often', says Miss Prism). In the light of what became public knowledge a few weeks later, Wilde's reference to the Savoy seems like sailing perilously close to the wind, and the author's own imprisonment lent a sad irony to Algernon's protest against being taken to Holloway: 'Well I really am not going to be imprisoned in the suburbs for having dined in the West End.' Elsewhere in the play as performed and published, only the defiantly unconventional use of the words 'immoral' and 'moral' echoes the deliberate flouting of conventional rules that marks Dorian and his mentor in Wilde's novel.

Bunbury Sources

William Green

William Green writes that the names Wilde uses in *The Importance of Being Earnest* fall into four categories: place names, such as Worthing (named after a seaside town); attributive names, such as Canon Chasuble (named after the liturgical garment); actual names, such as Lane, Algy's servant (named after Wilde's publisher John Lane); and purely fictitious names.

In an attempt to isolate the source of Bunbury, Green rejects the notion that it is a purely fictitious name or a place name. Green also dismisses the theory that Bunbury is an attributive name that connotes homosexuality. Green argues that Bunbury refers to two actual individuals: Henry Shirley Bunbury and Sir Edward Herbert Bunbury. Henry Bunbury knew Wilde when the playwright was a student at Trinity College. Henry was a part-time writer who, like the reference in the play, focused on his ill health. Sir Edward Bunbury was a geographer, a brilliant upper-class social gadfly, and a Greek scholar—attributes that appealed to Wilde.

William Green is a professor of English at Queens College, Flushing, New York. He is the author of *Shakespeare's Merry Wives of Windsor* and a contributor to numerous periodicals.

Wilde's fascination with names led him to utilize a variety of nomenclature techniques. These fall into four primary categories: place names, attributive names, the names of people of his own day, and purely fictitious names. All categories appear in *The Importance of Being Earnest,* and all bear examination before returning to the Bunbury question.

Place names particularly appealed to him. Worthing, the seaside town where Wilde lived while writing *The Importance of Being Earnest,* furnished him with the inspiration

Excerpted from "Wilde and the Bunburys," by William Green, *Modern Drama,* vol. 22, 1978. Reprinted with permission from *Modern Drama.*

for naming his male lead Jack Worthing. Lady Bracknell, the final appellation of that wonderful character, is named after Bracknell, the country residence of Lady Queensberry where Wilde had been a visitor. [Wilde biographer] Frank Harris reports Wilde once told him that "Territorial names have always a *cachet* of distinction; they fall on the ear full toned with secular dignity. That's how I get all the names of my personages, Frank. I take up a map of the English counties, and there they are. Our English villages have often exquisitely beautiful names. Windermere, for instance, or Hunstanton." (Although much of Harris's biography of Wilde is now considered suspect, I see no reason to doubt this particular story, supported as it is by evidence in the plays.)

Another kind of name which interested Wilde was the attributive. Canon Chasuble in the play obviously takes his name from the liturgical garment. Miss Prism, in [English essayist and poet, Samuel Johnson] Johnsonian humours fashion, refracts the light of learning.

Wilde did on occasion model his characters on people of the day, sometimes giving them new names, sometimes retaining the individual's own name. Lane, Algy's servant in *The Importance of Being Earnest*, is a direct hit at John Lane, Wilde's publisher. The two disliked each other, and Wilde showed the intensity of his feelings by using the name for a servant.

As a variation of this technique, we find near the end of the play buried in the group of names cited by Jack as he searches the Army Lists for his father's name, the unusual one of Maxbohm. This, it has been suggested, undoubtedly derives from [English essayist and caricaturist] Max Beerbohm, whom Wilde first met in 1893. Beerbohm was an occasional butt for Wilde's witticisms. For example, "When you are alone with him, Sphinx," Wilde once asked his good friend Ada Leverson, "does he take off his face and reveal his mask?"

Of course Wilde also employed purely fictitious names. So far as I can ascertain, Cecily Cardew is such an example.

The Source of Bunbury

To which category of names does Bunbury belong: invented, invented-territorial, attributive, or actual? Since each has a basis for laying claim to Bunbury, all are worth examining in establishing the case for the one I believe proper.

Perhaps there is no more mystery to Wilde's calling his phantom character Bunbury than that the name is fictive. It fits the characteristics Wilde wrote [acquaintance of Wilde, Abrey] Richardson he sought in a name. There is music in its long trisyllabic structure, with the internal alliteration, and the action-impelling quality of the plosive "b's." And "a memory of romance" and "suggestion of wonder" for the author of *The Happy Prince* as it rings the changes on "Ride a cock horse to Banbury Cross."

What about the possibility of Bunbury as an attributive name? Its characteristics are clearly spelled out in the play. On the simplest level, it signifies leading a double life. The dualism becomes more complex as a geographical connotation is given the term. One must travel somewhere to Bunbury, and the trip takes the Bunburyist from city to country to see a particular individual. How delightfully Wilde describes a Bunburying expedition of his own in a letter to his friend the criminologist George Ives, written almost certainly before *The Importance of Being Earnest:* "Dear George, I am charmed to see you are at the Albany—I am off to the country till Monday. I have said I am going to Cambridge to see you—but I am really going to see the young Domitian, who has taken to poetry!" (The Albany, incidentally, was Jack Worthing's town address in the play.) The highest connotative level of Bunburying is the moral. Here seriousness and frivolity are opposed to each other. From this level scholars have had a field day in interpreting the interlocking thematic commentary and the satiric barbs Wilde was launching against Victorian society.

Now, Wilde had been exposed to conceptional pseudonyms and nicknames with literary overtones from his earliest days. His mother, the poetess Speranza. His Oxford friends Bouncer and Kitten—William Ward and Reginald Harding respectively. Ada Leverson, The Sphinx. While we know why or how these individuals—and others—in Wilde's circle got their special names, I cannot find any lexical or literary evidence that would explain a similar origin for Bunbury. Nor do I believe in a play on the word *bum,* posterior.

HOMOSEXUAL CONNOTATIONS OF THE NAME BUNBURY

One theory has been advanced that would definitely classify Bunbury as an attributive name from the Victorian era. A few years ago an unidentified book reviewer for *Time* magazine stated that "Bunburying was shorthand for a visit to a fashionable London male whorehouse" and suggested that the word *bunburying* is related to *berging*—"the disguise of homosexual material in literature." I suspect this definition has its origin in details brought out at the trials about Wilde's own double life in which he shuttled between Alfred Taylor's male whorehouse and the brilliant world of Victorian high society. Undoubtedly it represents a post-*Importance of Being Earnest* linking of biographical information with the double life connotations of the play's Mr. Bunbury.

The homosexual vocabulary of the day does not support an earlier dating for such a definition. [Wilde scholar] Rupert Croft-Cooke, with his expertise in the lifestyle of Wilde and his circle, pinpoints four words particularly associated with the vocabulary of London's Victorian homosexual world: *so*, the equivalent of today's *gay* or *queer; renter*, a term describing a youth for sale; *queen*, still current; and *camp*, a word which then was used exclusively by sophisticated homosexuals.

Even allowing for the possibility that the term may have existed in the form of a private joke, Wilde had ample opportunity to avoid using it in the play if he suspected it had any homosexual connotations which might have drawn attention to him. Already when he was working on the script in August, 1894, Wilde knew the Marquess of Queensberry was on the rampage over his relationship with Queensberry's son, Alfred Douglas. Moreover, when making the name changes for the three-act version in preparation for production. Wilde could have substituted another name for Bunbury.

Further evidence to reject this homosexual connotation comes from the reviews of the original production. Surely if the Bunbury name had a homosexual overtone to it, some critic would have caught it. Yet the reviewers, when they mention the Bunbury material, call attention to it only as highly successful farce. And among these reviewers were George Bernard Shaw, H.G. Wells, William Archer, and A.B. Walkley. Thus any attributive quality and/or homosexual nuances to the name must be dismissed.

Let us now consider Wilde's predilection for invented-territorial names. Bunbury is a place—a village in Cheshire. Thought to be of Saxon origin, the village was at one time part of the huge Manor or Bunbury, which included twelve townships. Located near Calveley and about twelve miles southeast of Chester, Bunbury is today—and has been for centuries—a backwater, as my own recent visit confirmed.

It does not even appear on most maps. Thus Wilde's comment to Frank Harris that Oscar selected character names by taking up "a map of the English counties" would almost assuredly have not yielded the village Bunbury from such a source. Wilde, moreover, tended to restrict his territorially inspired character names to places where he actually had stayed. And the primarily agricultural, non-tourist, non-vacationer community of Bunbury does not appear to be one of them.

BUNBURY BASED ON HENRY SHIRLEY BUNBURY

If not derived from a place name, the final possibility is that Bunbury is based on an actual individual with this surname who in his lifestyle suggested sufficient traits to have served as the namesake of his dramatic counterpart. Bunburys flit through nineteenth-century English and Irish literary, social, and scientific worlds like butterflies. Could one be pinned down as Wilde's Bunbury?

"My father gave me to understand that it was he whom Wilde had in mind," writes the late Walter Bunbury in a letter I discovered among the papers of Reverend Maurice Ridgway, former Vicar of Bunbury. The letter continues: "We are an Irish family and at the time when young Wilde was at Trinity College, Dublin my father, then in his twenties, was living with a relative in Merrion Square only a few doors away from the Wildes' home. He had frequent invitations to Lady Wilde's 'salons' and often ran into young Oscar coming home from Trinity." Walter Bunbury never mentions his father by name in the letter; however, having located Walter's widow, Kathleen M. Bunbury, I learned from her that the father's full name was Henry Shirley Bunbury.

Henry Shirley Bunbury was born in Waterford, Ireland, about 1843. He was educated in England, and entered the Inland Revenue department of the British Civil Service in 1863. He remained with Inland Revenue until his retirement somewhere around 1907. During his career he was stationed in various cities in the British Isles. Although the record is not clear, it does appear that he was in Dublin during most of the time Oscar was at Trinity. In 1876, he was transferred to Monmouth. The last definite link between the two men is a letter Bunbury wrote to Wilde in 1878 congratulating him on winning the Newdigate Prize at Oxford. After his retirement, he went to Canada, then to Cuba, and died somewhere in the Caribbean about 1923.

Nothing in this sketch gives any hint of why he might have remained in Wilde's memory when Oscar was working on *The Importance of Being Earnest.* He did have elements of a double life in him, for while he earned his living as a government tax official, he was quite interested in literature. At the age of twelve he completed a tale of medieval knighthood entitled *The Error Corrected,* which was published in 1856. And I have been given to understand that he was a minor poet whose works were published in the local newspapers wherever he was stationed, although I cannot verify this.

There is a much stronger link between Wilde's Bunbury and Henry Shirley than this tenuous literary double life suggestion. In his letter to Canon Ridgway about his father, Walter Bunbury comments that at the time Henry was a regular visitor in the Wilde home: "my father was in rather poor health and inclined to discuss his physical troubles if given a chance. Oscar, I gather, enjoyed pulling his leg about this and often hailed my father with a jocular enquiry about his liver or lights. Although my father's health greatly improved later on he seldom failed to find some ground for complaint." These statements about Henry's health match up with the one concrete character trait Wilde has given his imaginary Bunbury: ill health. "I have invented an invaluable permanent invalid called Bunbury," remarks Algernon early in the first act, and allusions to Bunbury's illness are repeated several times in that act.

Why Henry Bunbury never revealed his probable role in the creation of Wilde's character is pure conjecture. All his son can suggest is that "[f]or some reason, my father was averse from disclosing that he was probably in Wilde's mind at the time the play was written. Although he had an ample sense of humour, he took his state of health with some seriousness, and would not at all [have] enjoyed being regarded as an imaginary invalid." Perhaps the reason was that by the time Henry knew of the play, Wilde was already in disgrace and Henry saw no point in raising the issue. After all, no one in the theatergoing world had detected this possible personal allusion to a Dublin acquaintance from twenty years in the past. A few years later, Wilde—a broken man—was dead, and soon after that Henry emigrated to North America.

BUNBURY BASED ON SIR EDWARD HERBERT BUNBURY

But the story does not end here, for while Henry Shirley Bunbury is the primary model, there is, I believe, a sec-

ondary one. He is Sir Edward Herbert Bunbury of Barton
Hall, Suffolk, ninth baronet of the line. He is distantly related
to Henry Shirley Bunbury through their common ancestry
with the Bunburys of Cheshire. (The family took the name
from the Manor of Bunbury where they had settled after
coming to England in the Norman invasion.)

Edward Herbert Bunbury was a graduate of Cambridge,
where he attained distinction in Classics. He became a barrister and also served as M.P. for Bury St. Edmunds for five
years. In 1886, upon the death of his brother, he succeeded
to the title. An exceptionally learned man in the arts and sci-
ences, he died a bachelor at the age of eighty-four, just a few
weeks after the opening of *The Importance of Being Earnest.*

It was as a classical geographer that Sir Edward became
best known. At the young age of twenty-eight he was elected
a Fellow of the Royal Geographical Society, and later served
on its Council for two years. His geographical writings consist of highly praised articles in the important English scientific encyclopedias of the nineteenth century, a continuous
outpouring of pieces on the classical world in the *Contemporary Review, Edinburgh Review, Quarterly Review* and
Fortnightly Review, and a definitive book. His two-volume *A
History of Ancient Geography* appeared in 1879, with a second edition in 1883. It is an amazing study of the mathemat-
ical geography and scientific cartography of the Greeks,
readable by specialist and layman. It was considered of such
major importance that the Royal Geographical Society presented Bunbury with a special resolution at its 1880 meeting
in appreciation of his accomplishment. When Dover Publications reprinted it in 1959, Professor W.H. Stahl, who wrote
a new introduction, commented that it is considered "the
standard work in English by virtually all scholars who have
labored in this field. . . . To go beyond Bunbury is to work
with the original Greek and Latin texts, many of which have
not been translated into English."

Bunbury's reputation was well established in scientific and
scholarly circles. His private life, however, he kept to himself.
His obituary in the *London Times*—he died March 5, 1895—
in an unusually long account notes that "even few of his com-
parative intimates realized the vast range of his knowledge
and the rare versatility of his gifts." This evaluation was
echoed in other obituaries of the day and seems to sum up the
public impression of Sir Edward Herbert Bunbury.

There is much about him to have attracted Wilde. Sir Edward was one of the Suffolk Bunburys known for their "brilliant social qualities and influential connexions"; in other words, of the upper class which Oscar so admired. In the country, his estate was at Barton Hall; in London, he lodged in St. James's Street. His writings emphasize travel. His own life was carefully separated into public and private compartments. Apparently these were kept well apart, as his obituary accounts indicate, giving him an aura of a double life. Again and again, we find overtones of Sir Edward in the imaginary Bunbury and in the character associated with him. And there was his reputation as a Greek scholar, not a characteristic reflected in Wilde's Bunbury, but one which would have had an impact on Oscar.

It is all too easy to forget that Wilde was a brilliant classicist himself, especially in Greek studies. And he never lost his interest in the ancient world. He maintained a lifelong acquaintanceship with his classics professor at Trinity, the Rev. John Pentland Mahaffy, acknowledging Mahaffy in a letter conjecturally dated April 1893 as "the scholar who showed me how to love Greek things."

Whether Mahaffy and Edward Herbert Bunbury may have been acquainted is unknown. However, they should have been aware of each other's writings. And it may have been through Mahaffy that Wilde became aware of Bunbury. In 1877, only two years before the first edition of Bunbury's *History of Ancient Geography* appeared, Wilde had travelled to Greece with Mahaffy. With the trip still fresh in his mind, one wonders whether Oscar would have been able to ignore the publication of such a major work of classical scholarship.

He was especially known—as his friends have commented —for his fabulous talent in picking up and retaining details about people, places, and things. Vincent O'Sullivan, for example, recollects, "He must have had a fund of information about many interesting people of the nineteenth century, things told him and things he had observed himself." The artist Sir William Rothenstein, also a Wilde acquaintance, observed, "He seemed to have read all books, and to have known all men and women. Tell me about so and so, Oscar, you would ask; and there would come a stream of entertaining stories, and a vivid and genial personal portrait."

No evidence exists to establish a direct link between Sir Edward Bunbury and Wilde. But for the reasons I have

given, I find it hard to believe that Sir Edward was totally unknown to him. Moreover, although elderly, Sir Edward was
still active in his London circles at the very time Wilde began his London literary career. And what can be more infu-
riating in speculating on some relationship between the two
than to learn that the bottom motto on Sir Edward's coat of
arms (there are two) reads *esse quam videri*—"to be rather
than to seem"—which to a great extent is the thematic
essence of *The Importance of Being Earnest.*

Whatever knowledge of him Wilde may have found useful
when constructing his character Bunbury, it only enlarged
the portrait that Henry Shirley Bunbury had already suggested. In essence, I believe Wilde's Bunbury to be a com-
posite of Henry Shirley and Edward Herbert. The imaginary
Bunbury has something of both men in him. Could Oscar
have resisted the temptation of blending two flesh and blood
Bunburys?

BUNBURY AS A COMPOSITE OF SOURCES

The real ones hark back to his student days, to a more conventional period of his life. Perhaps Wilde was unconsciously on a sentimental journey of his own—Bunburying
back through time to an era when his life had such a different pattern to it. A speculative thought whose answer is beyond proof positive! Yet who can truly fathom the recesses of
the creative mind? Who can determine what has been stored
there undergoing transmutation while awaiting the day
some small detail should be called forth from the depths of
the creative unconscious to be used in a poem or a play?

In calling the character Bunbury, Wilde may have relied
on the name as sufficiently common to have passed in the
theater without anyone's suspecting a real person or persons
serving as models. That the appellation sprang forth solely
from his imagination, I think I have proven was not the case.

In the long run, identification of Bunbury neither en-
hances nor detracts from the charm and wit that have made
The Importance of Being Earnest the masterpiece it is. As
Wilde once wrote to Professor Edward Dowden (whom he
had known at Trinity) concerning a matter of pronunciation
in "The Rape of the Lock," "The point is quite a small one,
but I know you like small points; so do I."

The Language of the Dandy

Patricia Flanagan Behrendt

Patricia Flanagan Behrendt writes that Wilde empha-
sizes strong male bonds in all four of his social comedies: *The Importance of Being Earnest, Lady Windermere's Fan, A Woman of No Importance,* and *An Ideal
Husband.* In each play Wilde includes a dandy, a fop-
pish, vain character who uses humorous and clever
language to promote himself and manipulate others.
Behrendt argues that the dandy's humor not only disguises his hostile desire to dominate other characters,
but also works to manipulate the audience. Viewers
are caught in paradoxical feelings of appreciating the
humor but feeling disdain toward the subject and the
fact that they are laughing at ideas that are not inherently funny. An example of this is the humorous but
relentless attack on heterosexual relationships.

According to Behrendt, the aim of the dandy is to use
language to draw another into his influence. Hence, language becomes a form of intellectual seduction, like verbal
petting and teasing. The strongest seductions in *The Importance of Being Earnest* and Wilde's other social plays are
man to man, reflecting Wilde's homosexual subject matter.
Behrendt maintains that even the title contains a deep homosexual pun: The name Ernest is a reference to a French
word, Uraniste, an equivalent to the German Urning,
which means males with homosexual tendencies.

Patricia Flanagan Behrendt is an assistant professor of
theater at the University of Nebraska, Lincoln.

Most scholars concerned with understanding Wilde's aesthetics in the drama focus on the problems posed by the language
of his plays, and particularly by the epigrams and paradoxes,
which seem to evade analysis because they are purposefully

ambiguous, a factor which promotes the assumption that Wilde's aesthetics in *The Importance of Being Earnest* evade rational analysis. However, insight into Wilde's verbal technique in the play depends upon the recognition of two largely overlooked aspects of the language of Wilde's earlier plays: (1) the role of the language of the dandy as an embodiment of the spirit of homosexual Eros, which constitutes a serious subtext in Wilde's first three social comedies, and (2) the aggressive nature of the language of the dandy, which has clear analogues in sexual behavior. In the earlier plays and in the critical dialogues which precede them, the intense and possessive relationships Wilde consistently depicts between men underscore the importance of the theme of homosexual Eros in Wilde's thought and in his aesthetic development.

In the first three social comedies, much of the interest of the plot itself concerns bonds between males. In *Lady Windermere's Fan*, the relationship between Cecil Graham and Lord Darlington illustrates Cecil's possessive and jealous attachment to his older role model. In *A Woman of No Importance*, Lord Illingworth's desire to mold Gerald in his own image and likeness reflects the homoerotic overtones of the critical dialogues. Finally, in *An Ideal Husband*, the dandy Lord Goring proves himself a better friend to Lord Chiltern than any woman, including his wife. In the process, he delivers the dandy manifesto—which had been incubating quietly in the two earlier plays—in the form of a misogynistic speech to Lord Chiltern's wife in which he tells her that her only reason for being is to support her husband totally since, in the scheme of things, a woman's life means less than a man's. The startling revelation of his cruel attitude toward women calls into question the reason for the confirmed bachelor's hasty and casual proposal of marriage to Lord Chiltern's sister Mabel. The marriage, in fact, will secure his position with Lord Chiltern, to whom he has proved himself devoted. The seemingly happy ending of the play—with its restored marriage and with its promise of a future wedding —offers us a brief vision of the future in which the real bond of enjoyment exists between the two men who, together, revel in their own self-proclaimed superiority.

AGGRESSIVE LANGUAGE OF THE DANDY

Although the dandy is easily recognized as the embodiment of questionable morality in Wilde's works, the most significantly dark aspect of the psychology of dandy language remains unexplored in criticism. The self-promoting language of the dandy—which seeks to disconcert, to manipulate, to fascinate, to hold in thrall, to dominate—is, above all else, a highly aggressive language. It is a language which epitomizes the paradox implied in "teasing"; for teasing both tantalizes and torments. In Wilde's earlier plays the manipulative language of the paradox and the epigram is largely the language of the dandy who is also intellectually superior to the other characters.

Since Wilde has dispensed in *The Importance of Being Earnest* with the kind of plot that requires the machinations of the dandy, no clear dandy emerges as a superior manipulative intellect in the image of the earlier Lords. However, Wilde's distribution among the four principal characters of dandyisms, in language and behavior largely associated with his own persona in real life, suggests that Wilde as author is the dandy intellect manipulating characters and audience alike. In *The Importance of Being Earnest,* the predominance of dandy language, in which humor belies the desire to dominate and to control, yields a greater understanding of the dandy viewpoint than any of the other plays. The fact that the dandy's humor masks an aggressive manipulation of the listener undoubtedly accounts for the schizophrenic responses of reviewers and critics alike to the play at the time of its premiere as well as in the more recent past.

While admitting to being amused by the play, George Bernard Shaw, for example, reveals a sense of anger at having been manipulated by Wilde's comedic style:

> It amused me, of course; but unless comedy touches me as well as amuses me, it leaves me with a sense of having wasted my evening. I go to the theatre to be moved to laughter, not to be tickled or bustled into it; and that is why, though I laugh as much as anybody at a farcical comedy, I am out of spirits before the end of the second act, and out of temper before the end of the third, my miserable mechanical laughter intensifying these symptoms at every outburst. If the public ever becomes intelligent enough to know when it is really enjoying itself and when it is not, there will be an end to farcical comedy.

Shaw reflects the discomfort of one who is uncomfortable with the fact that he feels both appreciation and disdain simultaneously. His words describe the process whereby the pleasure of being affectionately teased gives way to anger at being tormented. Since these emotions have their analogues in sexual play, one can surmise that Wilde's libido may have been the driving force behind his aggressive and seductive comic flair.

AUDIENCE MANIPULATION

The ability of Wilde's style to provoke hostility and discomfort transcends time. Written half a century after Shaw's remarks, Mary McCarthy's review of a production of *The Importance of Being Earnest* reflects similar polar responses. After acknowledging her enjoyment of the play, she concludes with a rather remarkable and damning assessment. She suggests that this supposedly trifling comedy "has the character of a ferocious idyll" in which "selfishness and servility are the moral alternatives present." McCarthy's term "ferocious idyll" suggests the paradox of the play in which an aggressive (ferocious) subject matter is packaged in the benign form of a mere idyll. The words of Shaw and McCarthy both reveal an appreciation for the play which gradually gives way to the feeling that the play is not what it seems. Both imply that mechanical laughter conflicts with the realization that, over the duration of the play, one has been duped into laughing at subject matter which is inherently not funny. In other words, one's laughter becomes a form of capitulation to something with which one might normally disagree. For example, when Algernon complains that at dinner he will have to sit next to Mary Farquhar who always flirts with her own husband, we laugh at his seemingly perverse inversions of conventions when he adds: "The amount of women who flirt with their own husbands is perfectly scandalous. It looks so bad. It is simply washing one's clean linen in public." By laughing at Algernon's observation, we reveal our recognition of the fact that he is inverting the true norm, which is that people flirt with those other than their spouses. Our laughter is a form of agreement or capitulation to the idea that a woman who flirts with her husband is unusual. Over the course of the play, Wilde offers a scathing view of heterosexual relationships and marriage to which the audience capitulates through what Shaw recognized to be mechanical laughter. Apparently, some members of Wilde's audiences historically, like those which included Shaw and, later, McCarthy, undoubtedly felt that through their own laughter they had been duped into playing a role in their own humiliation.

Another problematic concern for the student of Wilde is

the belief that the play contains homosexual themes which, while they are as difficult to pinpoint as the meaning of Wilde's paradoxes, contribute to the suspicion that audiences may be laughing at subject matter which they may not fully comprehend. For example, McCarthy suspected that

WILDE'S ATTEMPT TO RESTRAIN THE MARQUIS OF QUEENSBERRY

On February 14, 1895, opening night of The Importance of Being Earnest, *the marquis of Queensberry, outraged that Oscar Wilde befriended his youngest son, Lord Alfred Bruce Douglas, planned to expose the relationship by addressing the theater audience. Denied entrance, he angrily marched around the St. James Theatre accompanied by a prizefighter. Wilde instructed his lawyers to file suit; in response, the law firm of C.O. Humphreys, Son, and Kershaw replied that insufficient grounds existed to prosecute the marquis of Queensberry.*

We regret that we are unable to carry out your instructions to prosecute the Marquis of Queensberry for his threats and insulting conduct towards you on the 14th instant at the St. James's Theatre inasmuch as upon investigating the case we have met with every obstruction from Mr George Alexander, the manager, and his staff at the theatre, who decline to give us any statements or to render any assistance to you in your desire to prosecute Lord Queensberry and without whose evidence and assistance we cannot advise you to venture upon a prosecution. You personally would of course be unable to give evidence of that which occurred behind your back as to which you have no personal knowledge beyond information from others who apprised you of the insulting threats and conduct of his Lordship.

Had Lord Queensberry been permitted to carry out his threats you would have had ample ground for instituting a prosecution against him, but the only consolation we can offer to you now is that such a persistent persecutor as Lord Queensberry will probably give you another opportunity sooner or later of seeking the protection of the Law, in which event we shall be happy to render you every assistance in our power to bring him to justice and thus secure to you future peace at his hands. We are, dear sir, yours faithfully

C.O. HUMPHREYS, SON, & KERSHAW

"C.O. Humphreys, Son, & Kershaw to Wilde," a letter in Rupert Hart-Davis, ed., *More Letters of Oscar Wilde.* London: John Murray, 1985, pp. 129–30.

the pun of Wilde's title—*The Importance of Being Earnest*—which confuses the name Ernest with the concept of being "earnest," was not the only significance of the word play. In fact, she implies that the name must have a significance to which only a few are privy when she concludes, finally, that the "audience is pointedly left out of the fun" because "the joke about the name Ernest is doubtless a private one."

Eric Bentley muddied the literary waters further when he was asked to name the most significant piece of "gay theatre." He replied, "*The Importance of Being Earnest* because it is by Oscar Wilde and his best play." Here Bentley implies that the play reflects Wilde's nature by osmosis and leaves us to ponder how Wilde's homosexuality actually materializes in the work. Historically, of course, the play has lent itself to a variety of high camp interpretations on the stage. The most familiar camp tendency is to turn the characterization of Lady Bracknell into a transvestite role, a choice which vaguely implies that the play inspires experiments with gender which hint at homosexual appeal. For the most part, the homosexual content of the play has evaded critical analysis. However, understanding the role of the dandy in the earlier plays as the embodiment of homosexual Eros illuminates the homosexual subject matter in *The Importance of Being Earnest.*

INTELLECTUAL SEDUCTION

In the earlier plays, the amorally charming dandy's aim was to use his full powers of language to draw another character into his sphere of influence and to convince that character of the rightness of the dandy's vision of the world, which is highly critical of Victorian moral convictions. The effort is one of intellectual seduction accomplished through verbal petting and teasing. In these plays, the dandy's most emotional relationship is with another man who shares his vision of the world. For a time within the play the two criticize society, particularly relations between the sexes, from the self-proclaimed exalted position of the outsider—a position analogous to that of the intellectual and artistic homosexuals whose homosexuality was repudiated by Victorian society. Wilde's triumph as an artist was that theatre audiences were charmed by the stage dandy, a character whose behavior in real life they might recognize—but rarely acknowledge openly—as homosexual. Speaking through his characters in *The Importance of Being Earnest,* Wilde pursues the same critical views of Victorian society, particularly those concerning relations between the sexes, set forth in the earlier plays. The laughter of the audience is a measure of the degree to which he has manipulated them into accepting the dandy's vision of their own faults. Their laughter is an acknowledgement of his intellectual superiority, and by extension—though they are unaware of it—an acknowledgement of the superiority of the cult of the green carnation.[1]

While *The Importance of Being Earnest* perpetuates the dandy's vision of the ridiculousness of relations between men and women as it had been put forth in the earlier plays, it simultaneously reveals a matrix of allusions to the complex problems of homosexual identity. The title, which is traditionally interpreted as a pun on the importance of being Ernest as well as earnest, embodies a pun of a far more significant nature. Karl Heinrich Ulrichs (1825–95), a German sexologist who studied the phenomenon of homosexuality, applied the term *Urning* to males with homosexual tendencies, a condition which he felt reflected a female spirit in a male body. Proof that Wilde was familiar with one English equivalent of *Urning*—Uranian—is his use of the term in a letter to Robert Ross. More important, however, considering Wilde's expertise in French and his familiarity with things French, is the fact that, while the English equivalent of *Urning* is Uranian, the French equivalent is *Uraniste*—a term whose pronunciation clearly suggests the name Ernest. The fact that Wilde was probably familiar with the French term suggests that the title of his play may not only propose the importance of being Ernest or earnest but may also propose the importance of being *Uraniste* as well—a sentiment which refers to the intellectually superior role that Wilde had assigned to his dandies throughout his work, to the private delight of the coterie of the green carnation.

1. The green carnation was an emblem worn by homosexuals.

CHAPTER 2

Characterization in *The Importance of Being Earnest*

READINGS ON
THE IMPORTANCE
OF BEING EARNEST

Duplicity in *The Importance of Being Earnest*

Joseph Bristow

Joseph Bristow writes that *The Importance of Being Earnest* is structured around deceit, mistaken identities, and reversals of relationships. In short, people are never what they seem, and Bristow concludes that this makes it very difficult for the audience to gain psychological insight into the characters. In the play verbal trickery obscures motives and the audience focuses on *what* the characters say rather than *why* they say it.

Bristow argues that the deceptions of the two male characters, Jack and Algernon, mirror each other; Jack needs to escape the country for London's revels while Algernon feels that he must escape London for the solace of the country. According to Bristow, the country represents peace and innocence while the city stands for sociability, entertainment, and danger. As the play unfolds, the characters are constantly escaping to one place or another. The deceit and instability of the characters induce the audience to ask serious questions about the nature of earnestness, authenticity, and trust.

Bristow also discusses Wilde's use of food and eating in the play as a symbol of rapaciousness and duplicity. For example, when Algernon eats all of the cucumber sandwiches laid out for tea, the sandwiches symbolically represent both the hallmark of Lady Bracknell's snobbish society and sexual desire.

Joseph Bristow teaches at the University of York, England. He is the author of *Robert Browning, Empire Boys, and Sexual Sameness: Textual Differences in Lesbian and Gay Writing.*

Earnest starts and finishes with the hilarious relationship between two young bachelors whose identities, as the play progresses, grow more and more confused. At the outset, it is not entirely clear how and why these young men have come to know one another. In the first act, they meet in Algernon's opulent London flat. They loudly share jokes as if they were the best of friends. Obviously, they are enjoying the pleasures of high Society (the capital letter signalling, as it did in Wilde's day, the most luxurious life to be had). This is, indeed, a world of exceptional privileges: lashings of champagne, lavish parties, and the proprieties of high tea. Social rituals are certainly uppermost in their minds. In fact, among the first of the many ceremonies they lightheartedly discuss is courtship. 'Ernest' will soon be engaged to Algernon's cousin, Gwendolen. The odd thing is, 'Ernest' has been hiding his true identity from Algernon. Why?

This puzzling question is partly answered in the opening scene—with all sorts of implications for what turns into a very complex but perfectly fashioned plot. 'Ernest', it would seem, provides Jack with an excellent alibi: 'My name is Ernest in town and Jack in the country'. Jack, posing as 'Ernest', is leading a somewhat precarious double life. In his country seat, he is obviously known to everyone by his real name, Jack Worthing. However, since he finds his life on his estate constraining, and relishes the 'pleasure' of London society, he has had to devise another identity for himself. This, his alter ego, allows him to spend as much time as possible in the city. It is a complex ploy. To maintain these two identities, Jack tells different lies to different people. To his family in Hertfordshire, he claims that he has to go to London to see his irresponsible brother, 'Ernest'. When Jack reaches London and mixes with Algernon, he actually becomes the 'brother' he is supposed to be visiting. The country bores Jack; the city excites 'Ernest'. Only now, it seems, has he been found out. In the first scene, Jack is trying hard to explain to Algernon why he has different names in different places. Jack (alias 'Ernest') anxiously declares: 'I don't know whether you will be able to understand my real motives'. Although his motives may be hard to grasp, it becomes clear that this deception is a very careful piece of plotting.

DECEIT AND VERBAL TRICKERY IN THE PLAY

Mistaken identities; subtle deceptions; rapid reversals in relationships: these form the substance of Wilde's agile comedy. Confusions between names and faces, as well as names and places, hereafter proliferate. In each of its three acts, the play turns its attention to all sorts of amusing structures of deceit. Throughout *Earnest*, people are never quite what they seem to be. For a start, they do not even seem to correspond with what we might expect of dramatic characters. If they are not deceiving one another, then they are talking in a way that hardly seems authentic. They quip, joke, and come out with ideas and expressions that would appear to be something other than their own. It is, indeed, difficult to find some kind of psychological insight into either Jack or Algernon or anyone else in the play for that matter. It is *what* they say, rather than *why* they are saying it, that captures our attention. Inventive word-play; brilliant dialogue; sparkling wit: these are the things which drive the drama forward. Their motives vanish behind the brilliant façade of verbal trickery.

Even in the opening scene, the levels of intricate deceit begin to multiply. 'Ernest' is not the only character who adopts a persona to disguise his identity when he goes in search of 'pleasure'. Algernon, too, plays a similar trick upon his own relations. Just as Jack has invented the imaginary 'Ernest', so does Algernon have his fictional alias, 'Bunbury'. Like 'Ernest', 'Bunbury' makes enormous demands upon his inventor. 'Bunbury', according to Algernon, is 'an invaluable permanent invalid'—and so Algernon's endless visits to 'Bunbury' would appear to be the actions of a kind-hearted individual. At least, that is how Algernon wants to be understood. 'Bunbury', with his chronic illnesses and ceaseless calls on Algernon's attentions, enables Algernon to 'go down into the country' whenever he so wishes. For some reason or other, Algernon frequently needs to make a quick escape from London. Again, we are not exactly clear why.

JACK AND ALGERNON'S DESIRE TO ESCAPE

In a sense, Jack's and Algernon's means of deception mirror each other. The country-dweller (Jack) desires to escape to the city, and the city-dweller (Algernon) makes haste for the open country. The country and the city represent completely opposed values. In the country, there is peace, solitude, innocence—and boredom. The city, by contrast, is noisy, sociable, sophisticated—and dangerous. Whenever the country becomes boring, the city is duly entertaining. And when the city becomes too demanding, the country serves as a retreat. Given the extremely deceitful lives both Jack and Algernon indulge in, it is hardly surprising that the play should be punctuated with numerous frantic exits and entrances. People shuttle back and forth between the country and the city with remarkable speed. Practically everyone, for some reason or other, feels the urge to vanish into another world where, it may be inferred, they really ought not to be. And they try to make their escapes as quickly as they can. This impulse to flee from their supposedly proper places certainly gives rise to a great many complications which tie much of the action in entertaining knots.

Jack is the one who seems most keen to escape in the name of 'pleasure', and the more we find out about him, the stranger he seems. He has, to say the least, an unusual family background. Jack is certainly not any ordinary member of the landed gentry. Indeed, his only relation is his ward, Cecily, who is not that much younger than himself. Although heir to an estate, Jack has not inherited his wealth through a line of blood. As we discover in the final scene, Jack was adopted by Sir Thomas Cardew who found him, as an abandoned baby, inside a handbag left in a cloakroom at Victoria Station. He became Sir Thomas's adopted son. Jack, therefore, assumes he is an orphan. But only he, and not Cecily (the late Sir Thomas's daughter), knows the strange circumstances concerning his doubtful origins. Even then, he still does not know what his real identity was before he had the name, Jack Worthing, conferred upon him. In a far from inspired moment, Sir Thomas called him Worthing (a seaside resort in Sussex) because he happened to have a first-class ticket for Worthing in his pocket at the time. By the third and final act, this question of names is resolved. Jack, then, goes through a series of transformations. The man who first of all pretends to have a brother called 'Ernest', and tells his London friends he is 'Ernest', actually discovers, after many sudden reversals in the plot, that he really *is* Ernest. And by becoming truly Ernest in the end, Jack finds out that he is Algernon's brother. In other words, once falsely 'Ernest', Jack is eventually *Ernest* in *earnest*. The drama closes as soon as it has made dramatic sense of this pun.

This comedy, therefore, centres on what might appear a rather laboured play on words—with entirely unexpected consequences. Living a double life has, paradoxically, enabled the revelation of the far-fetched truth that 'Ernest' is, indeed, Ernest. Having sorted out who's who in the furious closing moments, we can see how *Earnest* elegantly turns upon two remarkable ironies. First, a man who has tried to deceive another turns out to be that man's brother. Second, a true identity (Ernest in earnest) is, simultaneously, a linguistic joke (E(a)rnest). Set up first as a manipulative *fiction*, 'Ernest' is ultimately a *fact*—but only through the workings of a most contrived piece of plotting. Given the strenuous lengths to which this piece of word-play on 'E(a)rnest' is taken, it should be abundantly evident that there is some point to it. It is not there just for the sake of fun. Indeed, all the jokes in *Earnest* have serious resonances to them. With this play on 'E(a)rnest' in mind, we can see how this lively and fast-moving comedy raises a number of related questions about who or what a person truly is. What is the difference between an authentic identity and a false one? When is 'Ernest' genuinely in earnest? To put this another way: who or what might be taken in earnest in *Earnest*? The significance of these questions will deepen as we witness the quick turn of dramatic events in detail.

THE RITUAL OF EATING

As soon as we discover how 'Ernest' and 'Bunbury' serve as 'covers' for each of the young men, the action swiftly changes, and the imperious Lady Bracknell and her daughter, Gwendolen, sweep on to the stage. Already Algernon has signalled that his aunt is coming to tea. The butler, Lane, has laid the table with suitable things to eat: cucumber sandwiches for Lady Bracknell, and bread and butter for Gwendolen. The trouble is, Algernon finds the cucumber sandwiches irresistible. In fact, he is in danger of eating them all up before his aunt arrives, and indeed he does. The sandwiches are important, for two reasons. Firstly, they are a hallmark of polite society. A proper high tea has to be graced with such delicacies. But secondly, and far less respectably, the sandwiches are among the many edible items suggesting rapacious desires. *Earnest* makes a whole host of rather vulgar allusions to love, romance, and sexuality. At crucial and potentially embarrassing moments, the comedy turns to rituals of eating, and each of the many foods mentioned seems charged with sexual meaning. Cucumber sandwiches; muffins; bread and butter; tea-cake: every single slice points to the hungriest of sexual appetites. Food is where each character's frustrated wishes are indirectly expressed, and most of these wishes concern sex. In this very proper world of courtship, engagements, and sudden bursts of passion, food becomes the focus for all sorts of anxieties that cannot be expressed out loud. 'Gwendolen,' says Algernon, 'is devoted to bread and butter', while he is equally unable to stop eating the sandwiches his aunt expects to be served at tea. Noticeably, Jack's very first words to Algernon closely align 'pleasure' with 'eating'. These two things, thereafter, are never sundered. For example, Lady Bracknell reports that she has just eaten crumpets with Lady Harbury 'who seems ... to be living entirely for pleasure now'. . . .

WILDE'S PORTRAYAL OF HIGH SOCIETY

Stern in her propriety, Lady Bracknell makes a striking impact, and it is her lines that audiences are likely to remember more than any other character's. Her part demands to be played with high-handed grandeur. She is a formidable Society Lady who never deviates from her grave aristocratic bearing. High Society involves a round of meetings and engagements where the rich upper classes lead their lives of leisure: shooting-parties, hunts, balls, and, of course, the 'Season', when young debutantes are ushered into the adult world of courtship and marriage. It is Lady Bracknell's self-appointed mission in life to subject everyone to her unquestionable authority, especially in matters of decorum and etiquette. Pencil in hand, she is ready to take note of Jack's suitability as a potential son-in-law. On practically every count—income, property, land, and politics—he wins her favour, until, that is, the story of the ill-fated handbag unexpectedly drops, like a lead weight, into the conversation. As Lady Bracknell's haughty response signals only too clearly to us, the idea of being born in 'a handbag' represents the ultimate *faux pas* in this ridiculously snobbish world. Under absolutely no circumstances can a daughter of the rich marry the son of a handbag. Who knows where he might have come from? Apart from the farcical element in this exchange between Lady Bracknell and Jack, there is perhaps a more significant point to be taken into consideration here. Lady Bracknell's contemptuous manner clearly demonstrates that the upper classes think of their servants as little more than worthless possessions. A servant, like a handbag, has a menial function. Neither is fit to marry a member of Society. The way this joke is handled would suggest that Wilde disagrees with the principles on which a class-divided society is based. But this is no ordinary society: it would clearly be a mistake to think that the representation of the upper classes here is realistic. Instead, *Earnest* uses the conventions of farce to send up the mannered behaviour and moral hypocrisy that lie at the centre of this privileged world.

Speranza: The Mother Figure in *The Importance of Being Earnest*

Patrick M. Horan

Although the nature of motherhood is not a dominant theme in Wilde's fiction, Patrick M. Horan argues that it is nevertheless significant. Horan maintains that in most of Wilde's major works and particularly in his comedies he portrays a mother figure that parallels the playwright's own mother, Speranza. Speranza is the pen name of Wilde's mother, Lady Jane Francesca Elgee Wilde.

Horan writes that Wilde's mother figures are dualistic, representing Speranza's conventional artistic sides. In *The Importance of Being Earnest,* Wilde depicts a world devoid of compassionate fathers and traditional families. Jack must find a family before he can find happiness. In the play Jack finds two mother figures—Lady Bracknell and Miss Prism—who represent the dual sides of Speranza's personality.

Horan characterizes Lady Bracknell as the conventional side of Speranza: She demands that Jack act in accordance with the rules of society. Like Speranza, Lady Bracknell is verbally adroit, brilliant, and caustically witty. Horan asserts that Miss Prism represents the other aspect of Speranza, her artistic personality. She is a writer and a fervent moralist. In the climactic scene, Jack mistakenly identifies Miss Prism as his mother. According to Horan, when Lady Bracknell becomes his mother, Jack finds filial respect, just as Wilde respected Speranza's self-sacrifice for him.

Patrick M. Horan teaches English at Montclair State College, Upper Montclair, New Jersey. He is a contributor to numerous periodicals, including the *English Journal* and *Sondheim Review.*

Speranza once stated that "the drama is meant to represent, not a visionary world, but intense phases of actual life." Wilde's dramas follow this philosophy because he represented his life experience in them, at least in his portrayal of mothers. Wilde acknowledged that his fiction and drama were autobiographical when he wrote to Alfred Douglas that his art was "the great primal note by which I had revealed, first myself to myself, and then myself to the world" (*"De P,"* 895). He also emphasized that he made the drama a mode of personal expression (*"De P,"* 912). Wilde's "personal expression" is obvious in his plays, at least in his definition of motherhood.

The mother characters in Wilde's drama evoke aspects of Speranza's complex personality. Lady Wilde never wrote drama and, curiously, she never attended one of her son's productions. Nevertheless, she had as strong a theatrical flair as Wilde, and she naturally became a model for many of the female characters in his plays.

The nature of motherhood is not the main theme of Wilde's fiction. Yet, mother characters are significantly present in these works. Tellingly, Mrs. Vane (the mother character in *The Picture of Dorian Gray*) embodies almost all of Speranza's qualities, even though she plays a minor part in a novel populated primarily by male characters. Like Speranza, Mrs. Vane is a self-sacrificing wife who still respects her unfaithful lover and is devoted to her children and their social advancement. Moreover, Mrs. Vane is as Bohemian as Speranza: in her youth she was an actress, and she still enjoys making life melodramatic.

Speranza's presence is most obvious in Wilde's comedies: *Lady Windermere's Fan, A Woman of No Importance,* and *The Importance of Being Earnest.* The mother characters of these works (e.g., Mrs. Erlynne, Mrs. Arbuthnot, and Miss Prism) are "women with a past" who scandalize the other "civilized" characters and who exhibit aspects of Speranza's dualistic personality. In other words, they are both conventional and Bohemian. . . .

JACK'S SEARCH FOR A FAMILY

Wilde's last and most famous dramatic work, *The Importance of Being Earnest,* concerns a young man's quest to find his family and to affirm the importance of having a mother as well as being earnest. In this absurdist comedy, Wilde appears only to play with mistaken identities and to extol the eating of too many cucumber sandwiches. Throughout all this nonsensical action, however, the importance of filial duty is continually stressed. Once again Wilde depicts a world that is populated by concerned mothers and devoid of compassionate fathers. In actuality, there are no father figures in *Earnest*. We never see Gwendolyn's father Lord Bracknell, Jack's adopted father, or even the briefly mentioned cart driver Jenkins, who is reported to be the father of recently born twins.

Like *Lady Windermere's Fan*, the plot of *Earnest* is complex and complicated by mistaken identities and characters with past secrets. Jack Worthing, the protagonist, has two goals: to find his family and to marry the charming Gwendolyn Fairfax. In the beginning of the play, we learn that Jack has invented a wicked brother named Ernest who resides in the city. Under the guise of visiting his wayward brother Ernest, Jack may absent himself from his country home and enjoy life in the city. Algernon Moncrieff, Jack's cohort and city friend, has similarly invented an invalid friend Bunbury who resides in the country so that he may escape from the city whenever he likes. Both men fall in love; Jack wants to marry Gwendolyn, while Algernon eventually romances Cecily Cardew. Both women, however, will only marry men named Ernest. Moreover, Lady Augusta Bracknell, Gwendolyn's mother, will allow her daughter to marry Jack only if he acquires "some relations as soon as possible." Underscoring this plot, therefore, is Wilde's premise that Jack cannot find happiness until he finds a family.

Jack eventually discovers his identity through Cecily's teacher Miss Prism, who is also a writer of three-volume novels. Miss Prism confesses to Jack that she was once his nanny. One day she inadvertently switched Jack and her manuscript. She left Jack in a handbag in the cloakroom of Victoria Station and placed her manuscript in the perambulator. Lady Bracknell then discloses that this perambulator belonged to her sister. Consequently, Jack is her nephew and his real name is Ernest. Thus, through Miss Prism and Lady Bracknell, Jack discovers his identity. The play concludes as Miss Prism recovers her handbag and Jack discovers the importance of having a family as well as the importance of being earnest.

LADY BRACKNELL AND THE CONVENTIONAL SIDE OF SPERANZA

This famous absurdist comedy is actually partly autobiographical. The two mother figures in this play—Lady Bracknell and Miss Prism—are quite different. Taken together, they illustrate the dual aspects of Speranza's personality. Lady Bracknell appears only in two scenes, but she is undoubtedly the most memorable character in the play (if not in Wilde's oeuvre). Originally Wilde named her Lady Lancing and underscored her importance by titling his first version *Lady Lancing*. She then was named Lady Brancaster; finally, Wilde called her Bracknell, which was the title of the estate owned by [Wilde's lover] Bosie Douglas's mother. Riichard Ellmann suggests that a bit of Lady Bracknell finds its source in Speranza's sister Emily Thomazine, who was an army wife and who always disapproved of Speranza's Bohemian ways. Yet Lady Bracknell also resembles that conventional, socially conscious side of Speranza.

Lady Bracknell gives voice to Speranza's belief that one should act in accordance with the rules of society. Consequently, she warns her nephew Algernon to "never speak disrespectfully of Society. . . . Only people who can't get into it do that." She disapproves of Jack as a potential son-in-law primarily because he is an orphan and therefore can never be socially influential. Conversely, she is proud of the dandy Algernon Moncrieff because he is an extremely "ostentatiously eligible young man. He has nothing, but he looks everything. What more can one desire?"

Lady Bracknell obviously differs from Mrs. Erlynne and Mrs. Arbuthnot because of her domineering, cantankerous personality. She is not a "woman with a past" nor is she a self-sacrificing, submissive housewife. Yet, like Speranza (and these early dramatic mothers), she is committed to making her child happy. Jack may call Lady Bracknell's attempts to secure a husband for Gwendolyn those of a "gorgon," but clearly she only wants her daughter to have the best possible marriage. Consequently, Lady Bracknell is fiercely determined to make sure that her child's husband is socially influential and wealthy enough to provide for her.

Wilde exaggerates Lady Bracknell's desire to create an ideal marriage for her daughter, in part, to undermine Speranza's notion that marriages should be ideal. For instance,

Lady Bracknell states of Mary Farquhar that "She is such a nice woman, and so attentive to her husband. It's delightful to watch them." Yet Algernon has already subverted this notion when he told Jack that Mary Farquhar's flirtations with her husband are unpleasant and indecent. Algernon concludes, "The amount of women in London who flirt with their own husbands is perfectly scandalous." Nevertheless, Lady Bracknell apparently shares Speranza's notion that attentive women make perfect wives. Thus, she quests for the perfect son-in-law because she believes that marriages should be ideal, even though her own marriage is far from this. Tellingly, she contrasts her marriage to Lord Bracknell with the Farquhar's "idealistic" relationship when she informs Algernon that her husband is used to dining upstairs.

[Literary critic] Alan Bird aptly concludes that Lady Bracknell unites 'the qualities of wit and social observation." For example, she announces to Cecily that "no woman should ever be quite accurate about her age. It looks so calculating." Wilde must have considered his mother's vanity and her practice of not being "quite accurate" about her own age when he gave this dictum to Lady Bracknell.

LADY BRACKNELL'S CHARACTER

Lady Bracknell clearly shares Speranza's verbal dexterity and adheres to her theory that "Epigram is always better than argument, . . . and paradox is the very essence of social wit and brilliancy." She displays Speranza's caustic wit when she replies to Jack's confession that he has lost both his parents by stating, "To lose one parent may be regarded as a misfortune. . . . [T]o lose both seems like carelessness."

Yet, Wilde had already portrayed witty mothers in his earlier works. For example, Mrs. Erlynne exhibits Speranza's talent for sarcasm when she announces that "there is a great deal of good in Lord Augustus. Fortunately it is all on the surface. Just where good qualities should be." Furthermore, she tells Lord Windermere that she is "Twenty-nine when there are pink shades, thirty when there are not." Undoubtedly, she resembles the vain Speranza who always greeted her guests with red shades drawn and candles lit even in midafternoon. Invariably, Mrs. Erlynne uses clever epigrams to captivate her listeners as well as to gain the affection of Lord Augustus. Even Herodias shares Speranza's flair for using paradoxes. For instance, she states, "I do not believe in miracles. I have seen too many."

When Speranza's friend, the Comtesse de Bremont, once called someone "a most respectable woman," Speranza answered, "Never use that word here. It is only tradespeople who are respectable. We are above respectability." Mrs. Vane in *Dorian Gray* echoes Speranza when she tells her son James that "Solicitors are a very respectable class, and in the country often dine with the best families." Similarly, Lady Bracknell sarcastically tells Jack that three addresses "always inspire confidence, even in tradesmen."

When Wilde originally wrote *Earnest* he never intended Lady Bracknell to be quite so gorgonlike. She became the stereotyped domineering and antagonistic mother-in-law in George Alexander's "reworked" version. In Wilde's original version, for example, Lady Bracknell (Brancaster) actually encourages Jack to find his identity and reads the army lists with him to find his father's name. In this original version, Lady Brancaster leaves for the station but returns at the end of the play to announce that she has missed her train and must stay with her family. Thus, Wilde surrounds her by a loving community of friends who have all become family members. Moreover, even in Wilde's existing text, the gorgonlike Lady Bracknell is evidently still a dedicated and devoted mother.

Wilde often expressed his unhappiness with [director and actor] George Alexander's editorial changes. For example, when he visited a rehearsal of the new version of *Earnest* that incorporated Alexander's suggestions, he stated, "Yes, it is quite a good play. I remember I wrote one very like it myself, but it was even more brilliant than this." Three years prior to this, Wilde had disagreed with Alexander about *Lady Windermere's Fan* because Wilde insisted that Mrs. Erlynne's identity as Lady Windermere's mother not be disclosed until the last act. Wilde reasoned that an audience would not understand a daughter being so disrespectful to her mother. Nevertheless, Alexander refused to accept Wilde's revisions. In short, Alexander was concerned with financial success; Wilde was concerned with presenting plays about dedicated mothers and respectful children.

MISS PRISM AND THE ARTISTIC SIDE OF SPERANZA

As Lady Bracknell evokes Speranza's conventional albeit sarcastically clever personality, Miss Prism represents her artistic sensitivity. Like Speranza, Miss Prism is a writer who has composed a three-volume novel. She is as dedicated to her novel as Lady Bracknell is to her daughter Gwendolyn. In a sense, she is a mother figure whose child is her art. For the sake of comedy Wilde has her switch the baby and the manuscript. Yet, this comic action also reveals her profound love for her "child," that is, her manuscript, which she lovingly wheels around in the perambulator. Miss Prism's respect for the written word is evidenced when she tells Dr. Chasuble that she cannot adequately state her feelings towards him, but she will forward him the last three volumes of her diary because in these volumes he "will be able to peruse a full account of the sentiments that I have entertained towards you for the last eighteen months."

Mrs. Erlynne and Lady Bracknell share Speranza's witty conversational ability; Mrs. Arbuthnot and Miss Prism, as her name suggests, evoke Speranza's puritanical moral fervor. Thus, Miss Prism concludes of the wayward Ernest,

> I do not think that even I could produce any effect on a character that according to his own brother's admission is irretrievably weak and vacillating. Indeed I am not sure that I would desire to reclaim him. I am not in favour of this modern mania for turning bad people into good people at a moment's notice. As a man sows so let him reap.

As evidenced by her conclusion that bad people should not be turned into good people at a moment's notice, Miss Prism shows that she also shares Speranza's talent for sarcasm. Furthermore, she is a realist who concludes of her novel that "The good ended happily, and the bad unhappily. That is what Fiction means." Overall, Miss Prism is as enigmatic as Speranza. She is capable of being both wickedly Bohemian and fervently puritanical. Consequently, we are told that she is both "a female of repellent aspect, remotely connected with education" as well as "the most cultivated of ladies, and the very picture of respectability."

In the climactic scene of *Earnest,* Jack mistakenly but proudly accepts Miss Prism as his mother. Miss Prism indignantly answers that she cannot be his mother because she is unmarried. Jack, voicing Wilde's feminist beliefs, states,

> Unmarried! I do not deny that is a serious blow. But after all, who has the right to cast a stone against one who has suffered? Cannot repentance wipe out an act of folly? Why should there be one law for men, and another for women? Mother, I forgive you.

This scene is characteristic of Wilde because it is as profound as it is comic. Jack reassesses his conventional beliefs about what a mother should be and is even willing to show filial duty to the unmarried Miss Prism. Jack never finds his real mother, but his former antagonist Lady Bracknell becomes his mother-in-law. Consequently, they are united in their shared quest to keep Gwendolyn happy.

Shortly after *Earnest* opened, Wilde was arrested and sent to Reading Gaol where he wrote his famous epistle *"De Profundis."* In this letter, he reaffirmed the importance of filial respect and once again thanked Speranza for her self-sacrificing actions.

Marriage and Women

Sos Eltis

Wilde revised *The Importance of Being Earnest* from four acts in the first draft to three acts in the final version. Sos Eltis argues that as Wilde revised the play his female characters became stronger and more original. In the early draft Gwendolen was a caricature marked by irritability and lack of dignity. In the final draft, Gwendolen is sophisticated, fashionable, self-possessed, and determined. Similarly, Cecily is transformed from a manipulative, cynical, and openly carnal female in the first draft to a natural, intelligent, and acute country girl in the final draft.

Eltis writes that Wilde also altered the relationship of the lovers. In the first draft both Cecily and Gwendolen are often ridiculed and presented as inferior to the men. For example, the men mock a woman's ability to acquire knowledge and education. By the final version of the play Wilde balances the sexes by having the men view their lovers with a humorous awe.

According to Eltis, a pervasive cynicism in the first draft is replaced with a carefree optimism in the final draft. This is best seen in Wilde's changed depiction of marriage. In the early draft marriage is portrayed as a monotonous financial necessity. In the final version marriage is more a fulfillment of romantic dreams—optimistic, sincere, full of energy, and happy.

Sos Eltis is a fellow in English at Brasenose College, Oxford. He is a specialist in nineteenth- and twentieth-century British literature.

As with all his previous plays, Wilde took *The Importance of Being Earnest* through a number of drafts to reach its final, apparently effortlessly witty, form. The first version of the play was immensely long, filling four exercise books with farcical accidents, broad puns, and a number of familiar comic devices.

Excerpted from *Revising Wilde: Society and Subversion in the Plays of Oscar Wilde*, by Sos Eltis. Copyright © 1996 by Sos Eltis. Reprinted with permission from Oxford University Press.

This manuscript was tightened and reshaped in successive drafts, and Wilde even continued to revise the play long after it had been performed, devoting much time to editing and proof-reading in order to perfect the final published version of 1899. This elaborate process of revision reveals the remarkable care that Wilde took with the play. Through each successive draft he gradually transformed it from a highly plotted, frequently absurd, but essentially harmless and familiar comedy into an insidiously subversive, satirical, and undeniably unique drama, a psychological farce. The existence of earlier versions of *Earnest* is more generally acknowledged than is the case with his earlier plays, primarily because it is known that Wilde complied with a request from [director and actor] George Alexander to cut the play from four acts to three. Much material had in fact already been excised before this apparently radical change, and the only major excision which resulted on this occasion was that of Algy's arrest for 'Ernest''s dining debts. Wilde characteristically concealed the meticulous attention he had already devoted to the play, complaining to Alexander that, 'This scene you feel is superfluous cost me terrible exhausting labour and heart-rending nerve-wracking strain. You may not believe me, but I assure you that it must have taken me fully five minutes to write!'. . .

THE TRANSFORMATION OF GWENDOLEN

Wilde's revisions produced more radical and unconventional roles for *Earnest*'s female characters, transforming them through successive drafts into stronger and more original individuals. The poised, independently minded Gwendolen starts life as a caricature bluestocking. Her pursuit of learning is either ridiculed as irrelevant, or reduced to a display of female vanity. So, in a childish squabble, Algy mocks Gwendolen's learning, while she defends herself in distinctly ambiguous terms:

> ALGY: I don't care to talk about music to Gwendolen any longer. She has grown far too intellectual during the three months. She seems to think that music does not contain enough useful information.

> GWENDOLEN: Algy! how dare you be so impertinent? And you don't know anything about the University Extension Scheme at all: I never return from any one of their lectures without having been extensively admired.

Unlike the rather terrifyingly self-possessed young woman of the final version, the first Gwendolen is often reduced to

> ### WILDE SENDS ALEXANDER HIS NEW PLAY
> *Wilde submitted* The Importance of Being Earnest, *accompanied by a short letter, to George Alexander, actor and manager of the St. James Theatre. Alexander not only produced the play but acted in it, as well.*
>
> My dear Aleck [George Alexander], I have been ill in bed for a long time, with a sort of malarial fever, and have not been able to answer your kind letter of invitation. I am quite well now, and, as you wished to see my somewhat farcical comedy, I send you the first copy of it. It is called *Lady Lancing* on the cover: but the real title is *The Importance of Being Earnest.* When you read the play, you will see the punning title's meaning. Of course, the play is not suitable to you at all: you are a romantic actor: the people it wants are actors like [Charles] Wyndham and [Charles] Hawtrey. Also, I would be sorry if you altered the definite artistic line of progress you have always followed at the St James's. But, of course, read it, and let me know what you think about it. I have very good offers from America for it.
>
> Oscar Wilde, "To George Alexander," in Rupert Hart-Davis, ed., *Selected Letters of Oscar Wilde.* Oxford: Oxford University Press, 1979, pp. 125–26.

comic caricature. She delivers absolute statements and contradicts them in her next breath. Not only female learning but female intuition is mocked, as Gwendolen proudly declares at the end of the play: 'Ernest! my own Ernest! I felt from the first that you could have had no other name. Even all man's useless information, wonderful though it is, is nothing compared to the instinct of a good woman.' The first Gwendolen is a less dignified figure, but she is also a more disagreeable one. In the final version Jack's concern that Gwendolen might become like her mother in about 150 years is comic because the daughter's stylish command and quiet determination are clear echoes of her mother's domineering ways. In the first manuscript version this subtle hint is more broadly stated, as Algy assures Jack he will have no authority over his future wife, because 'Gwendolen has one of those soft yielding natures that always have their own way.' Algy defines the hypocritical power of the female, and Gwendolen is reduced to a bullying gorgon like her mother.

THE TRANSFORMATION OF CECILY

In the final version, Gwendolen is the sophisticated, fashionable woman of the town, while Cecily is the natural, un-

spoilt country girl. Much of the humour derived from Cecily's character springs from the contrast between her supposed maiden simplicity and her actual intelligence, self-
possession, and knowing acuteness. Wilde was not the first
dramatist to exploit the stereotype of the innocent country
maid to comic effect. In *The Palace of Truth* (1870), [English
dramatist and librettist] W.S. Gilbert presents a maiden,
Azema, whose country innocence is a thin disguise for her
sexually predatory intentions. Azema, 'whose manner is
characterised by extreme modesty and timidity', is forced by
the spell on the palace unconsciously to betray her true motives. On meeting Prince Philamir, she explains her own
hypocrisy:

PHILAMIR: I beg your pardon, but the furniture
Has caught your dress.

AZEMA: [*rearranging her dress hastily*]
    Oh, I arranged it so,
That you might see how truly beautiful
My foot and ankle are. [*As if much shocked at the exposé.*]

Gilbert's Azema is simply one stock character pretending to
be another stock character: she is the devious, sexually experienced woman assuming the guise of the pure and modest maiden. Wilde's Cecily offers a far more subtle combination of these character-types, a combination which
ultimately undermines the stereotypes themselves.

While being more in thrall to Miss Prism and her
guardian and less quietly in control of Algy, the early Cecily
is also a more manipulative and worldly character. Un-
scrupulously mercenary like so many of W.S. Gilbert's
women, she sweetly informs Algy that: 'The next morning I
bought this little ring in your name; and put it down to an account I have opened for you at a very artistic jewellers who
has such a nice shop in our little country town.' She is knowing to the point of being cynical, commenting that the dull-
ness of society is due to it having far more culture than conversation. As with the heartless Mrs Cheveley, her
engagement to Ernest was broken off because he suspected
her of flirting with a lord; in Cecily's case, however, the suspicion was unfounded, as she explains: 'Of course it wasn't
true at all. And even if it had been, Lord Kelso is unmarried.
And it was not likely that I should have taken any interest in
an unmarried man. It is so easy to take an unmarried man
at an unfair advantage.' In some ways the early Cecily is

more openly carnal than her successor. The first Cecily approves of Jack refusing Algy an invitation to dinner because: 'Two luncheons would not be really good for your brother Ernest. He might lose his figure.' Yet she is also more traditionally passive, waiting for Algy to make all the first moves and simply responding with enthusiasm to his advances. The first Cecily is a country innocent along the lines of [English comic dramatist William] Wycherley's Margery Pinchwife, who longs to exchange her enforced rural inexperience for more sophisticated and corrupt knowledge. So when Miss Prism leaves Cecily in Algy's company, urging her to pursue her studies, Cecily eagerly replies: 'By the time that you return I feel sure that I shall know very much more than I do at present.'

The final Cecily is remarkable in that she combines the sheltered upbringing of the typical country innocent with the self-possession and intelligent poise of the experienced woman-about-town. Without being cynical or worldly, she has sufficient self-assurance to make her intentions and desires quite clear; when Algy declares that he loves her 'wildly, passionately, devotedly, hopelessly', Cecily calmly replies: 'Hopelessly doesn't seem to make much sense, does it?'

It is this honesty and forthrightness which distinguish Cecily from similar theatrical models. The heroine of W.S. Gilbert's short play, *Sweethearts* (1874), for example, has much in common with Cecily. Gilbert's Jenny Northcott is an apparently self-possessed young woman, who frequently succeeds in disconcerting her enthusiastic suitor, Harry Spreadbrow. There are a number of similarities between the two plays, for both couples meet in a garden and both young men ask for a flower as a token from their beloved—Jenny responds by offering Spreadbrow a geranium in a pot, but finally gives him a piece of mignonette, while he gives her a rose. Jenny's self-possession, however, is all a sham. She is playing the game of the flirt, but misplays it and lets her suitor leave without bringing him to a proposal; when she realizes that Spreadbrow has left for India and is not coming back to submit himself to more of her teasing, she bursts into bitter tears of despair. It is precisely this coquetry which separates the two heroines and brings about Jenny's downfall. Gilbert's heroine is made to suffer for her manipulative ways. The second act witnesses her humiliation: thirty years later Spreadbrow returns from India to find Jenny an old maid, still reproaching herself for her lost love. Spreadbrow not only fails to recognize his former love, but has forgotten every detail of their courtship. Jenny can produce the rose he once gave her, carefully pressed in the leaves of her book, whereas Spreadbrow tells her that he proposed to a governess only a week after leaving her. Jenny having thus been suitably humbled, Harry takes pity on her, and their courtship is renewed, with the man now in the dominant position and the woman at his mercy.

Nothing could be further from Algy and Cecily's courtship, where every attempt at patronizing superiority on Algy's part is gently deflated by his beloved. Right from the start Cecily is quietly in control, so when Algy greets her as his 'little cousin Cecily', she disconcertingly replies, 'You are under some strange mistake. I am not little. In fact, I believe that I am more than usually tall for my age.' The relationship between Wilde's lovers is summed up by the early Cecily's response to the romantic gibberish Algy recites for her diary: 'The fact is that men should never try to dictate to women. They never know how to do it, and when they do do it, they always say something particularly foolish.'. . .

WILDE'S BALANCE OF THE SEXES

In the first draft of *The Importance of Being Earnest* Cecily and Gwendolen are far from being on equal terms with their men. Indeed, many of the jokes in the first manuscripts are at the expense of women and their aspirations to equality. Just as Gwendolen's bluestocking pursuits are mocked by Algy in the first manuscript version, so Cecily's education is, unintentionally, ridiculed by Jack. His very seriousness on the subject of female education renders it laughable. So Miss Prism relays his exaggerated ideals:

> Indeed, he remarked to me privately in the hall when you had gone upstairs for your hat, that he had always been of the opinion that true femininity could not be attained without a thorough knowledge of the foreign languages, mathematics, and the ascertained principles of Political Economy.

The first Cecily does not share her guardian's reverence for female learning; while laughing at male vanity, she gives a low estimate of the capacity of women to acquire significant knowledge: 'Men have always despised women for their ignorance. And nothing so impresses a man as when he finds out that a woman knows half as much as he does. He thinks so much more of the other half.' Women are not only inferior as regards knowledge, they are also a literary embarrassment. Cecily condemns three-volume novels as not simply unreliable, but as a weakness on the part of one sex and below the notice of the other, for they are books that, 'every woman writes nowadays, and that no cultivated man ever reads'.

In the first manuscript draft, Jack and Algy regard the opposite sex not with the humorous awe which characterizes later drafts, but with an air of cynical superiority. When Algy counts through the few relatives he does not hate, they all, apart from Gwendolen, suffer from a succession of female failings, for he likes 'Mary Farquhar, when she isn't chattering about her husband; and Gladys, when she isn't chattering about someone else's husband: and dear old uncle Geoffrey, who isn't half a bad sort in his silly way, considering what a thoroughly typical woman Aunt Augusta is.' What hope is there for the female sex if the awful Lady Brancaster is a 'typical woman'?

In successive drafts Wilde readjusts this balance between the sexes, until the two wield equal power and draw equal sympathy. If, in the final version, Cecily and Gwendolen take the initiative, it is to encourage Algy and Jack to pursue a course they already desire to follow. The young men are neither henpecked nor patronizingly superior; when Algy attempts any such pose, Cecily rapidly deflates it. Male domination is mocked as thoroughly as female education was in the first draft. In a statement, perhaps too obvious to escape Wilde's blue pencil, Miss Prism warns her pupil that: 'The fact is, you have fallen lately, Cecily, into a bad habit of thinking for yourself. You should give it up. It is not quite womanly. . . . Men don't like it.' The disapproval of the ludicrously old-fashioned and curiously opinioned governess is quite enough to endorse the ideal of female independence. Indeed, the very idea that men dislike women thinking for themselves confirms the threat it poses to their fragile claim to supremacy.

WILDE'S VIEW OF MARRIAGE

Wilde's revisions also edited out the note of cynicism which marked the earlier versions, and introduced instead the carefree optimism and charm which characterize the final version. So, in the first manuscript version, Cecily expresses the opinion that 'marriage, as an institution, was quite impossible unless the husband gave up to the wife in every single thing'. Cecily's resolution to assume a Lady Brancaster-like control over her husband links her closely to W.S. Gilbert's devious female leads. In *Engaged* (1877) the mercenary and manipulative Minnie Symperson disguises a cool business head under the simpering manners of the *ingénue:*

> Papa dear, I have thought the matter over very carefully in my little baby-noddle, and I have come to the conclusion—don't laugh at me, dear papa—that it is my duty, my *duty*—to fall in with Cheviot's views in everything *before* marriage, and Cheviot's duty to fall into my views in everything after marriage. I think that is only fair, don't you?

The characters of *Engaged* are lovers in no more than name, for marriage is simply a form of stock market where you wheel and deal to secure the largest share of available money for yourself. Their rapturous professions of love are simply the hypocritical language of greed. Earlier versions of *The Importance of Being Earnest* came closer to this, though Wilde's characters never sank to quite the same levels of hypocrisy. So, in early versions, Wilde's lovers are tainted by mercenary motives. The emphasis on Algy's debts suggests that he may share some of his aunt's interest in Cecily's fortune. Cecily and Gwendolen are driven by genuine desire for their respective Ernests, but even their motives are mixed, as their interrogation of Jack reveals:

> CECILY: We would naturally like to learn something about Ernest's personal appearance.
> GWENDOLEN: Any information regarding Ernest's income would be eagerly welcomed.

The first *Earnest* has much in common with the cynical world of *Engaged*. The earlier incarnations of the lovers regard marriage with world-weary cynicism, not as the fulfilment of their romantic dreams but as the mundane conclusion of a far more pleasant flirtation. In the final version Algy observes: 'It is very romantic to be in love. But there is nothing romantic about a definite proposal.' Algy's emphasis on uncertainty as the essence of romance is the last witty remnant of his and Jack's earlier disparaging views on marriage. So, in the first version, Jack does not wish to be a good husband as that sounds 'so tedious and second-rate'. Algy observes rather more fairly that: 'If a chap makes a good husband there must have been something rather peculiar about him when he was a bachelor. To be a good husband requires considerable practice.' He does, however, set the final seal on the married state by replying to Jack's enthusiastic eulogy over Gwendolen with the sceptical theory that 'all women are far too good for the men they marry. That is why men tire of their wives so quickly.' Nor is this critical attitude to marital bliss confined to the men; Gwendolen, too, informs Jack that, fortunately, she does not trust him, because 'If I could do *that*, I fear I would find you tedious.'

This view of marriage as monotonous, second-rate, but financially necessary is very much in line with the dark comedy of *Engaged*. The final version of *The Importance of Being Earnest*, however, paints a very different picture. It is Lady Bracknell alone who regards marriage firstly as a financial and social transaction, and secondly as a battle for domination. The young lovers have a considerably more optimistic view of the matter; their professions of love are sincere, and they persevere in the face of much opposition. Their relationships are, of course, influenced by the comic traditions of love at first sight, but the unusual outspokenness of the women and the comic determination of the men separate them from the automatic responses of convention. This separation between the lovers' and Lady Bracknell's views on marriage is important to the satirical thrust of the play. When Lady Bracknell's snobbery and mercenary greed stand in the way of genuine attachments they appear not merely ridiculous but pernicious. In just the same way, Gwendolen's obvious self-possession and strength of mind make her mother's insistence on ruling her life not just humorous but unjust. Lady Bracknell's declaration that, 'An engagement should come on a young girl as a surprise, pleasant or unpleasant, as the case may be' again underlines the division between her unnatural and old-fashioned approach to marriage and the happier, irrepressible energies of the younger generation.

The Importance of Being Earnest and Social Masks

Norbert Kohl

Norbert Kohl writes that the humor in *The Importance of Being Earnest* stems from the interplay between the seriousness of the situations and the characters' unexpected reaction to these situations. This clash of opposites, called the technique of inversion, is used to jolt the audience's expectations as the characters react frivolously to the serious emotions of love, grief, birth, and death. Kohl argues that Lady Bracknell's separation of emotion from intellect gives her an absurd perspective, as she continually focuses on superficial, rather than essential, matters. She represents the severe Victorian middle-class tradition of devotion to duty, a strict work ethic, and the hatred of idleness. Kohl maintains that the comic nature of Miss Prism also flows from an unexpected interplay, the contrast between her moral severity and the actual situation. In short, where she should be emotionally touched she lapses into moral righteousness.

Kohl suggests that Cecily and Gwendolen are characters dependent on a ritual of manners. For example, when it appears that both are engaged to the same man they mask their real feelings with exaggerated politeness and a façade of formality. According to Kohl, this artificiality permeates the play. The characters are more like puppets than actual people because they cover authentic emotional responses with the masks of social convention. Kohl argues that Wilde thus exposes the middle-class materialistic concerns and motives that lurk behind the masks.

Norbert Kohl is a professor of English Literature at the University of Freiburg in Breisgau, Germany.

It is understandable that theatre critics who were used to the plays of [English playwright Sir Henry Arthur] H.A. Jones, [English dramatist Sir Arthur Wing] Pinero, [Norwegian playwright Henrik Johan] Ibsen and [Irish dramatist George Bernard] Shaw should have found themselves somewhat disorientated by such a work, and inclined to throw up their hands in helpless protest rather than accept the challenge of something quite new in the history of English comedy. The anonymous critic of *Truth,* for instance, thought that any serious review of the play would be like investigating the ingredients of a soufflé after dinner. Even the famous critic William Archer regarded this 'absolutely wilful expression of an irrepressibly witty personality'—as he called the play—as being only the product of a fantasy that 'imitates nothing, represents nothing, means nothing, is nothing'. Following a dictum of [English critic Walter] Pater's, he set it in the context of music, calling it a *'rondo capriccioso,* in which the artist's fingers run with crisp irresponsibility up and down the keyboard of life'.

How Wilde runs up and down the 'keyboard of life' may already be seen from closer inspection of the title, which is perhaps the best starting-point for any interpretation. The obvious homonymic word-play between 'Ernest' and 'Earnest' is underlined by the sub-title, which is, 'A trivial comedy for serious people'. The earnest folk to whom the play is addressed are, of course, the Victorians, for whom the epithet is highly apposite. Devotion to duty, a strict work ethic, hatred of idleness—these were characteristic of the puritanical and evangelical traditions that marked the Victorian attitude to life. . . .

The irony of Wilde's title consists in the fact that the only earnest item in the play is the name Ernest—there is little sign of seriousness in the situations or the characters. The verbal irony of the title continues logically and consistently throughout the action, with earnestness being trivialised and the name Ernest being taken seriously. Cecily and Gwendolen set so much store by the name that they make their choice of marriage partner dependent upon it. On the other hand, Lady Bracknell considers Jack's being found in a hand-bag as nothing but a cause for reproach that he should have shown such contempt for the 'ordinary decencies of family life'; she is not in the least interested in the extraordinary fate of such a foundling. By focusing on this violation of the 'decencies', she reduces a potentially pathetic situation to a mere breach of social etiquette, and life to a question of style. Gwendolen sums up the priorities that apply to this whole play: 'In matters of grave importance, style, not sincerity, is the vital thing'.

Wilde opposes Victorian earnestness with a philosophy of the surface, which his sub-title denotes with the word 'trivial'. This is his conceptual counter to 'serious' and 'earnest', and carries connotations of intellectual and moral detachment from reality, concentrating on the inessential and insignificant surface of things. His view of the trivial is expressed in *De Profundis:*

> The trivial in thought and action is charming. I had made it the keystone of a very brilliant philosophy expressed in plays and paradoxes.

WILDE'S COMIC TECHNIQUE

The contrast between the trivial and the serious, as expressed in the sub-title, and the punning irony of the name Ernest coupled with the quality of earnestness, prefigure the comic effect of the play. The irony and the comedy arise primarily from the continual interplay between, on the one hand, an intellectual and trivialising perspective of events and situations that seem to demand an earnest, emotional response or conformity to social propriety, and on the other hand an earnest and ponderous way of looking at things that are trivial and external. This constant clash of opposing perspectives results in the reader's or spectator's habitual expectations for ever being punctured. The method governing this continual alienation of reality by way of the artistic imagination at play is the principle of inversion. This becomes the behavioural norm, while paradox is its verbal expression. The role of the sexes, for instance, is reversed in the matter of courtship: when Jack wishes to propose to Gwendolen, he stutters to a halt, and she has to take the initiative; similarly, Algernon—so experienced in 'Bunburying' —learns that for three months, as can be proved by her diary, Cecily has already cast him as her fiancé. The comedy of this scene, however, does not reside solely in the fact that the action springs from Cecily, but also in the parody of 'love at first sight', an ever-popular romantic theme. Imagination does not follow reality, but anticipates it, in accordance with the paradoxical thesis of Vivian in 'The Decay of Lying': 'Life imitates art far more than Art imitates life.'

In this apparently weightless, light-hearted world of fantasy, where Jack wears mourning because of the death of a non-existent brother, while his friend Algernon is simultaneously pretending to be the brother as he declares his love to Cecily, the laws of Nature are flouted as blatantly as those of everyday life. Nothing is safe from the playfulness of the intellect—the emotions of love and grief, and the objective extremes of birth and death. Even these are deprived of their factualness and become subject to the whims of the subjective viewpoint, being unexpectedly transformed into malleable phenomena. When she hears from Algernon that Bunbury is dead, after the doctors had discovered that he could no longer be alive, Lady Bracknell responds:

> LADY BRACKNELL: He seems to have had no great confidence in the opinion of his physicians. I am glad, however, that he made up his mind at the last to some definite course of action, and acted under proper medical advice.

What matters to Lady Bracknell is not the fact of Bunbury's death but the fact that he 'acted under proper medical advice'. Conventional expectations are thereby stood on their head, since Bunbury apparently did not benefit from this advice but simply died. It is even conceivable here that this paradox represents a satirical jibe at the deficiencies of medical practice in Wilde's day. But what matters above all to Lady Bracknell is social propriety. In a form of cross-examination satirising the conventional Victorian approach to marriage, she questions Jack about his age, income, property in town and country, political beliefs and origin. After learning, to her consternation, that he has lost both parents—which she regards as a sign of 'carelessness'—and appears to have no relations at all, as he was found in a hand-bag, she urges him 'to make a definite effort to produce at any rate one parent, of either sex, before the season is quite over'.

LADY BRACKNELL AND SOCIAL CONVENTIONS

Lady Bracknell's worship of rank and title, respectability and social prestige makes her the classic figure of social snobbery and narrow-mindedness. She shakes her head to hear that Jack lives on the 'unfashionable side' of Belgrave Square, and in her arrogance she embodies that stratum of society which Wilde himself could never reach, however much he loved to bask in its glamour. This was the meeting-place of rigid conservatism, philistinism, and dandified aestheticism. In no other character is the separation of emotion from intellect, already a feature of characterisation in the earlier comedies, so consistent and so dominant as in Lady Bracknell. She regards sympathy with invalids as 'morbid', and tells Algernon to ask the sick Bunbury to avoid a relapse on Saturday if possible, as she has arranged the last dinner-party of the season for that day and would like Algernon to attend. There is a fine example of this mixture of Victorian conventionality and aesthetic alienation in the scene where Jack kneels in order to propose, and Lady Bracknell enters unexpectedly:

> LADY BRACKNELL: Mr Worthing. Rise, sir, from this semi-recumbent posture. It is most indecorous.
>
> GWENDOLEN: Mamma! [*He tries to rise; she restrains him.*] I must beg you to retire. This is no place for you. Besides, Mr Worthing has not quite finished yet.
>
> LADY BRACKNELL. Finished what, may I ask?
>
> GWENDOLEN: I am engaged to Mr Worthing, mamma. [They rise together].
>
> LADY BRACKNELL: Pardon me, you are not engaged to anyone. When you do become engaged to someone, I, or your father, should his health permit him, will inform you of the fact. An engagement should come on a girl as a surprise, pleasant or unpleasant, as the case may be. It is hardly a matter that she could be allowed to arrange for herself . . .

Lady Bracknell does not ask why Jack is kneeling, and she is not concerned with her daughter's feelings towards him. All that matters to her is the visitor's extraordinary posture, and her sole purpose is to restore social decorum. What is basically a serious situation is rendered ridiculous by the formal perspective through which she views it, and the visual comedy of the tableau is underlined by the rigid formality of the language. The dignified stiltedness of Lady Bracknell's dialogue effectively shatters one's expectations of a spontaneous emotional reaction. Jack's kneeling position is viewed neither as the unbearable servility of a potential marriage candidate, nor as a symbolic, pre-marital exchange of roles, but it simply arouses her repugnance because it clashes with her idea of what is 'decorous'. The absurdity of this perspective, which concentrates on the surface and not on the essence, serves to throw a satirical light on the Victorian convention of parents deciding on their children's choice of partner. All too often the daughter's emotions counted for less than the financial situation of the wooer, and here as elsewhere in the play Lady Bracknell becomes the mouthpiece for such conventions. When later on, for instance, Jack reveals that his ward Cecily has a fortune of about £130,000, Lady Bracknell suddenly finds Cecily a 'most attractive lady'.

MISS PRISM'S EMOTIONAL DETACHMENT

A character like Lady Bracknell, whose urbanity barely disguises her relationship to the matchmaker of classical comedy, stands out as a comic figure primarily because she combines Victorian conventions with aesthetic attitudes. The latter throw into relief the deficiencies of the former, so that in laughing at her, the predominantly middle-class Victorian audience could scarcely avoid also laughing at themselves. There is a similar incongruity of perspective to be observed in Miss Prism, Cecily's governess and the authoress of a lost three-volume novel 'of more than usually revolting sentimentality'. Unlike Lady Bracknell she brings a more moral tone to her insistence on propriety. Her Christian name, Laetitia, stands in ironic contrast to the stiff conformity of her conduct and the sententious nature of her somewhat affected language—already hinted at by her surname, which suggests a combination of 'prim' and 'prissy'. The superficiality of her ostentatious respectability is evidenced by her response to the news of Ernest's death: 'What a lesson for him! I trust he will profit by it.' The paradox of this reaction lies in the fact that she regards Ernest's dissolute life style as being responsible for his death, and so death should now inspire him to a greater insight into his own wrongdoing. Just how a dead man is supposed to see his own death as a punishment, and profit from the insight, is left unclear. The triviality of her attitude lies in the grotesque clash between her moral severity and the actual situation.

There is a similar reaction when Jack asks her to identify the hand-bag in which he was found:

> MISS PRISM [calmly]: It seems to be mine. Yes, here is the injury it received through the upsetting of a Gower Street omnibus in younger and happier days. Here is the stain on the lining caused by the explosion of a temperance beverage, an incident that occurred at Leamington. And here, on the lock, are my initials. I had forgotten that in an extravagant mood I had had them placed there. The bag is undoubtedly mine. I am delighted to have it so unexpectedly restored to me. It has been a great inconvenience being without it all these years.

While Jack waits in great suspense for her answer, she proceeds to go into all the minute details when, in the context, one would simply have expected her to say whether or not this really is the bag she lost twenty-eight years ago in Victoria Station. And even after she has at last confirmed that the bag is hers, she does not say a single word about the all-important fact that this clears up the mystery of Jack's origins. The 'injury', the stain and the initials are not regarded as clues to the existential significance of the bag, but merely evoke memories of the past. Jack's agony of suspense is in stark contrast to Miss Prism's total disinterest in the fate of the baby she once deposited in the bag. Just as Ernest's death served only to inspire her to moral sententiousness, so too does this hand-bag episode leave her emotionally quite untouched—she seems to have completely shut out any sense of personal responsibility for what happened. Thus she trivialises a serious situation, ignoring both the fate of the child and her own part in that fate, and concentrating all her attention on one superficial aspect of the affair, which is the identity of the bag. This alone is worthy of 'earnestness'.

THE ARTIFICIALITY OF CECILY AND GWENDOLEN

Not all the characters succeed in replacing emotional involvement with intellectual detachment as completely as does Miss Prism; nor do they all conform to the social conventions of propriety as perfectly as Lady Bracknell. The long dialogue between Cecily and Gwendolen in Act 2, when they both realise that they appear to be engaged to the same man, is one instance where the protective coating of perfect manners is seen merely to be a cover for 'that dreadful universal thing called human nature':

> CECILY [*Advancing to meet her.*]: Pray let me introduce myself to you. My name is Cecily Cardew.
>
> GWENDOLEN: Cecily Cardew? [*Moving to her and shaking hands.*] What a very sweet name! Something tells me that we are going to be great friends. I like you already more than I can say. My first impressions of people are never wrong.
>
> CECILY: How nice of you to like me so much after we have known each other a comparatively short time. Pray sit down.
>
> GWENDOLEN: [*Still standing up.*]: I may call you Cecily, may I not?
>
> CECILY: With pleasure!
>
> GWENDOLEN: And you will always call me Gwendolen, won't you?

CECILY: If you wish

GWENDOLEN: Then that is all quite settled, is it not?

CECILY: I hope so [*A pause. They both sit down together.*]

Then they discover that they are apparently engaged to the same man:

> CECILY: Do you suggest, Miss Fairfax, that I entrapped Ernest into an engagement? How dare you? This is no time for wearing the shallow mask of manners. When I see a spade I call it a spade.
>
> GWENDOLEN: [*Satirically.*]: I am glad to say that I have never seen a spade. It is obvious that our social spheres have been widely different.

The excessive affection of the first dialogue is already rather suspect as it is so unmotivated. One would in fact have expected Gwendolen to be rather more reserved and indeed surprised to find such a pretty young girl in her fiancé's house. And shortly before meeting Gwendolen, Cecily had presumed that she must be 'one of the many good elderly women who are associated with Uncle Jack in some of his philanthropic work in London'. Both have good cause to be suspicious, but they mask their feelings with exaggerated politeness.

The exchange of elaborate courtesies is like a ritual whose ceremonial character is underlined by the symmetry of the movements. Cecily and Gwendolen move towards each other, shake hands, stand for a moment or two, and then sit down together. Once they have sat, both the physical and the verbal ceremonies of introduction are completed. In these symmetrical movements, which are also to be observed elsewhere in the play, [literary critic] Otto Reinert detects 'a kind of dance, slow and elaborate, a visual image of the artifice of sophisticated courtship and a major device in the play's esthetic distancing'. Gradually, ineradicable differences emerge, but at first the two young ladies retain their polite tone. Their adherence to the formalities laboriously holds up a façade which threatens at any moment to collapse. The stage directions reveal a formal parallel between their actions and their words. After Cecily has revealed that she is engaged to Ernest Worthing, they both rise 'quite politely' (Gwendolen) and 'very politely' (Cecily), and produce their diaries in order to prove their engagements. The tempo of the dialogue slows down: Gwendolen speaks 'meditatively', Cecily 'thoughtfully and sadly', but then it accelerates through such key words as 'entanglement' and 'entrapped', until it reaches a climax with the passage quoted. The ritual of manners is now denounced as a masquerade, though the masks are only laid aside for a brief moment. Gwendolen's barbed comment on their different social spheres wounds through satire and not through crude insults or ranting complaints. The entrance of servants immediately exercises a 'restraining influence' on the two girls, who then proceed to talk in the most formal terms about town and country life, while nevertheless firing little arrows at each other through the formality.

The symmetrical gestures and movements express an artificiality that permeates the whole play and indeed links it together. It becomes an artistic mode of alienating reality, with the characters at times appearing almost mechanical, like puppets rather than people. As well as shaping the dramatic situation, as in the rivalry and reconciliation of Acts 2 and 3, for instance, or in the final tableau of the three couples embracing, the symmetry and parallelism also shape the dialogue, which abounds in repetitions and inversions. When the two young ladies realize that the supposed Ernest is actually Algernon, and Ernest alias Jack is really John, they react so uniformly that they no longer seem to be individuals:

GWENDOLEN: My poor wounded Cecily!

CECILY: My sweet wronged Gwendolen!

This reduction of individuality, and hence of possible variation, is conveyed by the syntactic parallel which has a comic effect as described by Bergson: 'du mécanique plaqué sur du vivant'. The process is taken one step further in the chorus at the beginning of Act 3:

[*Gwendolen beats time with uplifted finger.*]

GWENDOLEN AND CECILY [Speaking together.]: Your Christian names are still an insuperable barrier. That is all!

JACK AND ALGERNON [Speaking together.]: Our Christian names! Is that all? But we are going to be christened this afternoon.

MOTIVES BEHIND THE SOCIAL MASKS

Of all the formal techniques, however, the most potent in this play is the paradox. As the stylistic pendant to the constructional principle of inversion, it systematises the counter to orthodox opinion. It arises from the desire to disconcert the partner by way of the unexpected formulation. Effect is all, and at times one has the impression of being confronted by perfect rhetorical specimens, each little gem exquisitely prepared and mounted. But the paradoxes cannot simply be dismissed as cheap effects, for in many instances they serve to explode established conventions, thereby exposing to view those aspects of reality that had hitherto been cloaked by existing norms. In Act 1, for instance, Lady Bracknell and Algernon are talking about the widowed Lady Harbury, whose husband died fairly recently:

> LADY BRACKNELL: I'm sorry if we are a little late, Algernon, but I was obliged to call on dear Lady Harbury. I hadn't been there since her poor husband's death. I never saw a woman so altered; she looks quite twenty years younger.
>
> ALGERNON: I hear her hair has turned quite gold from grief.

The reader or spectator is not surprised that Lady Harbury has been altered by her husband's death, but he certainly does not expect her to have become younger or to have hair that has turned 'quite gold from grief'. The conventional cliché of the grieving widow, ageing and with even more grey hair than before, is quite shattered by Wilde, who depicts a rejuvenated woman 'who seems . . . to be living entirely for pleasure now'. The substitution of 'gold' for the expected 'grey' is particularly effective, for the unconventional and unnatural change of hair colour may also allude to the inheritance which the pleasure-loving widow is now enjoying. Such paradoxes illustrate vividly how social decorum is to be seen merely as a mask of conformity, and they also bring out the true motives that lurk behind the mask. Lady Harbury's inability to mourn, thanks to the golden days that now lie ahead of her, may be seen as a parallel to Lady Bracknell's evaluation of Jack and Algernon as candidates for the hands of Gwendolen and Cecily—their suitability being judged in accordance with their incomes. Emotions such as grief and love have no place in either case. Materialistic considerations are all-important, and morality is reduced to a matter of business.

CHAPTER 3

Philosophy, Themes, and Meaning in *The Importance of Being Earnest*

READINGS ON
THE IMPORTANCE
OF BEING EARNEST

Wilde's Attack on Seriousness

Philip K. Cohen

Philip K. Cohen, a Wilde scholar, writes that *The Importance of Being Earnest* defies classification because it contains elements of romantic comedy, comedy of manners, farce, parody, and burlesque, all of which trivialize the serious things in life and treat trivial matters seriously. Cohen argues, however, that a fairy tale atmosphere dominates the play. Like fairy tales, the play moves unfettered from reality to a world of wish fulfillment. According to Cohen, Wilde mixes daydreams and reality so the two become indistinguishable. Young and old alike expect life to conform to their desires, however unrealistic. Cohen concludes that in this fantasy world Wilde attacks the seriousness of the human condition and pain and death are robbed of their power. Only Bunbury suffers and dies, but he, of course, is imaginary.

The Importance of Being Earnest defies classification by means of traditional generic labels. It contains elements of romantic comedy, comedy of manners, farce, parody, and burlesque. The plot, in which two sets of young lovers overcome an elderly blocking figure to triumph in marriage, encompasses the traditional action of romance. And Wilde has neatly, symmetrically structured his romance plot. But the quality of wit and occasional satirical thrusts at high society ally the play equally with the comedy of manners. Yet the comedy of manners cannot comfortably contain its preposterously incongruous situations, its episodes so loosely strung on the thread of the romance plot, and its emphasis on these episodes rather than on character. These are the hallmark of farce. Of the possible generic classifications, the last mentioned coexists most congenially with fantasy, which dominates the play. Though *The Importance of Being Earnest* must certainly be considered unique, a far greater playwright had long before brought together the same elements in *A Midsummer-Night's Dream*. But the component of fantasy subserves in Shakespeare's play, whereas it presides unchallenged over Wilde's. He had to generate fantasy without the aid of such accomplices as Puck [a sprite in Shakespeare's *A Midsummer-Night's Dream*], and to make it reign supreme in the most inherently realistic of literary modes, the drama.

The play shows Wilde returning to the separate, subcreated realm of fairy tales, and to their license for fantasy. He had written of the stories constituting *The Happy Prince and Other Tales:* "The former are an attempt to mirror modern life in a form remote from reality—to deal with modern problems in a mode that is ideal and not imitative." Yet almost invariably he permitted the importunate, undisguised facts of the human condition to intrude upon and destroy the separate world of his tales. In *The Importance of Being Earnest,* however, he achieves a degree of remoteness from reality that unfetters fantasy and gives free rein to wish fulfillment. These triumph completely over the problems of modern life in general and Wilde's own life in particular. Reality enters the world of the play only to be disarmed—with laughter, rather than in battle. Whereas fairy tales have been viewed as vicarious rites of initiation, *The Importance of Being Earnest* issues a witty, humorous refusal to grow up. Jack would rather not be "christened along with other babies." Wilde supplies him with the perfect ironic reason: "It would be childish."

THE THEME OF TRIVIALITY

The play derives from the philosophy of Lord Goring [the eligible bachelor in Wilde's *An Ideal Husband*], Wilde's prototypal perpetual youth. It is, in fact, Wilde's generic tribute to Goring's outlook on life. Mabel Chiltern's [character in Wilde's *An Ideal Husband*] ideal husband paid an extraordinary amount of attention to the trivial matter of a buttonhole. Wilde clearly stated the philosophy of Goring—and of *The Importance of Being Earnest*—in an interview that appeared in *St. James's Gazette* on January 18, 1895: "we should treat all the trivial things in life seriously, and all the serious things in life with sincere and studied triviality." And he subtitled the play *A Trivial Comedy for Serious People*. Conventionally "serious people," of course, would dismiss the play as a mere "trivial comedy." But he knew that those seriously and sincerely dedicated to the trivialization of life's significant concerns would fully appreciate it. As Algernon points out, "one must be serious about something, if one wants to have any amusement in life." Wilde resolves this paradox by calling for a shift of commitment from important to inconsequential matters and, through this adjustment, a redefinition of significance itself. Thus, to be flippant about dinner at Willis's, for example, is to display a "shallow" nature. And an indiscriminately serious approach to everything indicates "an absolutely trivial nature." Meals matter very much, but serious "scrapes" are "the only things that are never serious."

In *The Importance of Being Earnest*, Wilde trivializes not only specific sources of anxiety in his personal life, but also

---

ABSENCE OF REALISM

In 1895 an anonymous journalist for London's St. James Gazette *interviewed Oscar Wilde about his new play* The Importance of Being Earnest. *Wilde declares that the play is a work of fancy with a philosophy.*

'Do you think that the critics will understand your new play. . . ?'
'I hope not.'
'I dare not ask, I suppose, if it will please the public?'
'When a play that is a work of art is produced on the stage what is being tested is not the play, but the stage; when a play that is *not* a work of art is produced on the stage what is being tested is not the play, but the public.'
'What sort of play are we to expect?'
'It is exquisitely trivial, a delicate bubble of fancy, and it has its philosophy.'
'Its philosophy!'
'That we should treat all the trivial things of life very seriously, and all the serious things of life with sincere and studied triviality.'
'You have no leanings towards realism?'
'None whatever. Realism is only a background; it cannot form an artistic motive for a play that is to be a work of art.'

"Mr. Oscar Wilde on Mr. Oscar Wilde" in E.H. Mikhail, ed., *Oscar Wilde: Interviews and Recollections,* vol. I. New York: Harper & Row, 1979, p. 250.

his own literary embodiments of his moral preoccupations. He exploits the license of farce for loose, episodic construction in order to produce encapsulated parodies of scenes, themes, and even passages in his other works. . . . Whereas previous protagonists lied and found themselves suddenly confronted with the potentially destructive truth, Jack discovers that he has been telling the truth all along, despite his best efforts to fib. His name *is* Ernest, and he *does* have a brother. When the truth comes out in *A Woman of No Importance* and *An Ideal Husband,* the protagonists must acknowledge it and beg forgiveness. In the denouement of *The Importance of Being Earnest,* Wilde turns the concept of forgiveness itself on end. The past, which poses a threat in the tragicomedies, resolves the problems in his last play as the revelation of Jack's identity overcomes Lady Bracknell's objections and assures the two marriages. Blessed with the discovery of a past that makes him more, rather than less, acceptable to others, Jack begs pardon for his unintentional virtue rather than for a sin: "Gwendolen, it is a terrible thing for a man to find out suddenly that all his life he has been speaking nothing but the truth. Can you forgive me?" His comment cannot be construed as a condemnation of the truth, which the play shows to be more functional than its opposite. The truth counts, not because of its inherent moral value, but simply because it works. Beyond this practical consideration—if, indeed, practicality can be deemed at all relevant to the play—the truth is trivial.

WILDE'S BLENDING OF REALITY AND WISH FULFILLMENT

Ways in which the play's structure and constituent episodes comment on Wilde's earlier works could be cited endlessly. Most are apodictic. But, like the majority of Wilde's works, *The Importance of Being Earnest* has more than one layer of meaning. Some of Wilde's self-escape takes place beneath the play's glittering surface. Jack arrives at his country estate in mourning clothes only to find himself confronted with the subject of his feigned grief. Here Wilde presents a humorous reworking of [Biblical king of Judea] Herod's relationship with Iokanaan. It has been shown that Herod's guilt and anxiety originate in the murder of his brother. Iokanaan represents to Herod a reincarnation of his victim and revivifies his conscience. Early in *The Importance of Being Earnest,* Jack proposes "to kill my brother." He arrives in the country confident that he has successfully executed this pseudo-crime. But Algernon, under the assumed identity of Ernest Worthing, confronts his murderer, temporarily disturbing the peace in Herefordshire. As in *Salome*, the corpse has in a way arisen from the dead. But in *The Importance of Being Earnest*, this unexpected resurrection, while it exposes a fib, also effaces the crime. Herod kills his brother and cannot escape the deed; Jack does away with an imaginary brother only to be rewarded with a real one. This farcical redaction of the psychological relationship between Herod and Iokanaan robs it of its moral significance.

Wilde includes in his attack against seriousness not just situations in his own life and works, but the human condition itself. Even suffering and death fall prey to his major weapon, fantasy. Although the action takes place in settings every bit as realistic as those in *Lady Windermere's Fan*, for example, the play makes no further concessions to reality. Wilde does not create an entirely fictitious and separate realm of experience, as do writers of fairy tales. But he so thoroughly entwines characters' wishful daydreams and the actual course of events that the two become indistinguishable. In fact, he makes life yield and conform to the characters' desires. Wilde alerts one to the absolute power of wishes early in the play. Algernon has planned to be Jack's guest for dinner at Willis's, even though he has not been invited and has a previous engagement with Lady Bracknell and the world of responsibility. He introduces his dinner plans casually and with full confidence that the future will meet his expectations:

> ALGERNON: If it wasn't for Bunbury's extraordinary bad health, for instance, I wouldn't be able to dine with you at Willis's to-night, for I have been really engaged to Aunt Augusta for more than a week.
> JACK: But I haven't asked you to dine with me anywhere tonight.
> ALGERNON: I know. You are absurdly careless about sending out invitations.

Algy seems blithely unaware of the possibility that reality might not accommodate his preconceptions. But such awareness is unnecessary in the play, for the afternoon's wish inevitably becomes the evening's event: Algy gets his supper. Gwendolen has decided to marry Jack even before they meet. Cecily has experienced the agonies and ecstasies of a vicissitudinous courtship and engagement with Jack's brother for a full eight months prior to their first meeting. Gwendolen marries the Ernest she has dreamed of, and Cecily's preconceived engagement issues in wedlock at the play's end.

THE CONFLICT BETWEEN FANTASY AND REALITY

Lady Bracknell, who represents the older generation and functions as the blocking figure in the romance plot, also believes that reality will respond without question or hesitation to her will. She authoritatively acquaints Gwendolen with the news that she is not, after all, engaged:

> Pardon me, you are not engaged to any one. When you do become engaged to someone, I, or your father, should his health permit him, will inform you of the fact. An engagement should come on a young girl as a surprise, pleasant or unpleasant, as the case may be. It is hardly a matter that she should be allowed to arrange for herself.

The older generation, too, fearlessly imposes its expectations on experience. And Wilde wants to convince the reader that these expectations, based on convention and tradition, are every bit as fantastic as the childish dreams of the young. Her seemingly impossible demand that Jack locate at least one parent by the end of the season—and the gratuitous manner in which he does exactly this—strongly recall the archetypal fairy-tale plot and underscore the shared function of fantasy in fairy tales and Wilde's highly original drama. Circumstances in *The Importance of Being Earnest* just happen to fulfill the wishes of both the young and the old, and thus to complete the vision of harmony and reconciliation that is Wilde's own fantasy.

As Wilde's fairy tales purposefully illustrate, fantasy cannot thrive in the presence of suffering and death. He therefore robs these adversaries of their power in the play. The imaginary Bunbury is in this sense the play's scapegoat. He alone suffers; and, despite all the talk of killing, only he dies. In the first act Algernon refers to the fictitious Bunbury as "a dreadful invalid"; later Lady Bracknell inquires about the health of her nephew's "invalid friend," who, she is pleased to learn, has had the good sense and strength of character to die. The word-play involved in this epithet conveys perfectly Wilde's point about suffering and death. The invalid who escapes the former through the latter is invalid, a pure fiction. Death, where is thy sting? In the fantastic ambience of *The Importance of Being Earnest*, the aging process can be reversed. Lady Harbury "looks quite twenty years younger" since her husband's demise. The clock stops ticking when Jack inquires if Gwendolen will become like her mother "in about a hundred and fifty years." Time, which not only ends life, but also belongs to the world of schedules, appointments, and responsibilities, bows submissively to fantasy. Only Lady Bracknell, the unconventional representative of convention, takes the clock seriously as she complains of having "missed five, if not six, trains." But her concerns yield to youth, which views a moment and a lifetime with equally majesterial indifference:

> JACK: I must retire to my room for a moment. Gwendolen, wait here for me.

> GWENDOLEN: If you are not too long, I will wait here for you all my life.

The perpetual children stand unawed by the grim reaper and the hourglass—both very trivial matters.

The Importance of Being Earnest as an Anglo-Irish Parable

Declan Kiberd

Declan Kiberd argues that *The Importance of Being Earnest* is, among other things, a parable of strained Anglo-Irish relations. For the Irish playwright the existence of a double throughout the play represents England and Ireland. Kiberd claims that Bunbury, Algernon's double who embodies all that is most creative and corrupt, represents Ireland. Ireland, like Bunbury, offers a convenient image of innocence and spontaneity yet presents an intractable problem for the repressed English society that mistakenly equated natural instincts with vice.

Kiberd also explores Wilde's cynicism toward the presumed virtue of sincerity, identifying it as a social mask. In the play each major character turns out to be his or her opposite, and gender roles are inverted—manly women do male things and womanly men do feminine things. Kiberd contends that Wilde further challenged the thinking of his day when he rejected the philosophy of determinism where birth, background, and upbringing preordain lives. Wilde fiercely defends the autonomy and changeability of the self, viewing it as artwork.

Declan Kiberd is professor of Anglo-Irish literature and drama at University College Dublin, Ireland. He is the author of many books, including *Men and Feminism in Modern Literature* and *Inventing Ireland.*

Wilde's art, as well as his public persona, was founded on a critique of the manic Victorian urge to antithesis, an antithesis not only between all things English and Irish, but also between male and female, master and servant, good and evil, and so on. He inveighed against the specialization deemed essential in men fit to run an empire, and showed that no matter how manfully they tried to project qualities of softness, poetry and femininity on to their subject peoples, these repressed instincts would return to take a merry revenge. [English critic and poet Matthew] Arnold's theory had been that the Celts were doomed by a multiple selfhood, which allowed them to see so many options in a situation that they were immobilized, unlike the English specialist, who might have simplified himself but who did not succumb to pitfalls which he had not the imagination to discern. Wilde knew that in such Celtic psychology was the shape of things to come.

Wilde was the first major artist to discredit the romantic ideal of sincerity and to replace it with the darker imperative of authenticity: he saw that in being true to a single self, a sincere man may be false to half a dozen other selves. Those Victorians who saluted a man as having 'character' were, in Wilde's judgement, simply indicating the predictability of his devotion to a single self-image. The Puritan distrust of play-acting and the rise of romantic poetry had simply augmented this commitment to the ideal of a unitary self. This, along with the scope for psychological exploration provided by the novel, may have been a further reason for the failure of nineteenth-century artists before Wilde to shape a genuinely theatrical play, [English poet Percy Bysshe] Shelley's *The Cenci* being far better as poetry than as drama. Wilde argued that these prevailing cultural tendencies also led to some very poor poems written in the first person singular: all bad poetry, he bleakly quipped, sprang from genuine feeling. In the same way, he mocked the drab black suit worn by the Victorian male—[German socialist Karl] Marx called it a social hieroglyphic—as a sign of the stable, imperial self. He, on the contrary, was interested in the subversive potential of a theatricality which caused people to forget their assigned place and to assert the plasticity of social conditions. Wilde wrote from the perspective of one who realizes that the only real fool is the conventionally 'sincere' man who fails to see that he, too, is wearing a mask, the mask of sincerity. If all art must contain the essential criticism of its prevailing codes, for Wilde an authentic life must recognize all that is most opposed to it.

WILDE'S USE OF INVERSION

In consequence, in *The Importance of Being Earnest*, each person turns out to be the Irelander turned Englander.

Whatever seems like an opposite in the play materializes as a double. For example, many critics have found in it a traditional contrast between the brilliant cynicism of the town-dwellers and the tedious rectitude of the rural people; but that is not how things work out. Characters like Canon Chasuble and Miss Prism are revealed to have contained the seeds of corruption and knowingness all along, while Cecily has her most interesting (that is, evil) inspirations in a garden (rather reminiscent of her biblical predecessor). So every dichotomy dichotomizes. Wilde's is an art of inversion and this applies to gender stereotypes above all: so the women in the play read heavy works of German philosophy and attend university courses, while the men lounge elegantly on sofas and eat dainty cucumber sandwiches.

Far from the men engaging in the traditional discussion of the finer points of the female form, it is the women who discuss the physical appeal of the men: when Algernon proposes to Cecily, it is *she* who runs her fingers through *his* hair and asks sternly: 'I hope your hair curls naturally. Does it?' (The answer is 'Yes, darling, with a little help from others.') When Algy rushes out, Cecily's instant response is: 'What an impetuous boy he is! I like his hair so much!' The last word on these inversions of gender roles is spoken by Gwendolen, when she praises her own father for conceding that a man's place is in the home and that public affairs may be safely entrusted to women:

> Outside the family circle, papa, I am glad to say, is entirely unknown. I think that is quite as it should be. The home seems to me to be the proper sphere for the man. And, certainly once a man begins to neglect his domestic duties he becomes painfully effeminate, does he not? And I don't like that. It makes men so very attractive.

It would be possible to see this cult of inversion as Wilde's private little joke about his own homosexuality, but it is much more than that: at the root of these devices is his profound scorn for the extreme Victorian division between male and female. A historian of clothing remarked in 1969 that, if a Martian had visited Victorian England and seen the clothes worn there, that Martian might have been forgiven for thinking that men and women belonged to different species. In the history of men's fashions over the previous four centuries, it was only in the Victorian age that men presented themselves with no trace of the 'feminine'. The Elizabethan gallant had been admired for his shapely legs, starched ruff and earrings; the Restoration rake for his ribbons, muff and scent; the Romantics for their nipped-in waists, exotic perfumes and hourglass shapes. Such details indicate that the androgyny of the male and female had never been fully suppressed.

Wilde always liked to create manly women and womanly men, as a challenge to the stratified thinking of his day. He had seen in his mother a woman who could edit journals and organize political campaigns in an age when women had no right to vote; and it was from her that he inherited his lifelong commitment to feminism. 'Why should there be one law for men, and another for women?' asks Jack of Miss Prism near the end of *Earnest:* if the double standard is right for men, then it is right also for women; and if it is wrong for women, then it is wrong also for men. Wilde demonstrates that the gender-antitheses of the age were almost meaningless: in the play, it is the women who are businesslike in making shrewd calculations about the attractions of a proposed marriage, while it is the men who are sentimental, breathless and impractical.

WILDE'S REJECTION OF DETERMINISM

By rejecting such antithetical thinking, Wilde was also repudiating the philosophy of determinism, that bleak late-nineteenth-century belief that lives are preordained by the circumstances of birth, background and upbringing, a conviction shared by a surprising range of the age's thinkers. The extreme sects of Protestantism had long believed in the notion of the elect and the damned, but radical critics such as Marx and Freud evolved secular versions of the theory, viewing the person as primarily the effect of childhood training and social conditioning. For these figures, environmental factors often overwhelmed the initiatives of the individual, a view summed up in the Marxian claim that consciousness did not determine social being but that social being determined consciousness. To Wilde, who believed in the radical autonomy of the self, this was hateful stuff. He saw the self as an artwork, to be made and remade: for him, it was society that was the dreary imposition. 'The real life is the life we do not lead'—that is, the one lived in pure imagination and in acts of playful dissent which deliver us from the earnestness of duty and destiny.

The Importance of Being Earnest challenges ideas of manifest destiny by the strategy of depicting characters reduced to automatons by their blind faith in the preordained. Gwendolen idiotically accepts Jack in the mistaken belief that he is Ernest: 'The moment Algernon first mentioned to me that he had a friend called Ernest, I knew I was destined to love you.' The whole plot machinery creaks with an intentional over-obviousness. Jack, for instance, says that the two girls will call one another 'sister' only after they have called each other many worse things as well, and this is exactly what happens. The women, perhaps because they seem to have been more exposed to Victorian education than the men, show a touching faith in determinism. Ever since Cecily heard of her wicked uncle, she talked of nothing else. Her faith, however, takes on a radical form, as she finds in it the courage to reject the tedious, all-female regime of Miss Prism and to bring her *animus* to full consciousness in the ideal Ernest, with whom she conducts a wholly imaginary affair before Algy's actual arrival. In doing this, she was already rejecting the notion of an antithesis between herself and others, because she had already recognized the existence of that antithesis in herself. Just before meeting her wicked uncle, she denies the idea of a black-and-white world: 'I have never met any really wicked person before. I feel rather frightened. I am afraid he will look just like everyone else.' Wilde insists that men and women know themselves in all their aspects and that they cease to repress in themselves whatever they find unflattering or painful. In abandoning this practice, people would also end the determinist tyranny which led them to impute all despised qualities to subject peoples. Anglo-Saxonist theory, as we have seen, insisted that the Irish were gushing and dirty by inexorable inheritance, and as unable to change any of that as they were unable to alter the colour of their eyes. But Wilde showed otherwise.

THE PLAY AS A PARABLE OF ANGLO-IRISH RELATIONS

The Wildean moment is that at which all polar oppositions are transcended. 'One of the facts of physiology', he told the actress Marie Prescott, 'is the desire of any very intensified emotion to be relieved by some emotion that is its opposite. The trivial comedy turns out, upon inspection, to have a serious point; the audience itself is acting each night and must be congratulated or castigated for its performance; and the world will be an imitation of the play's utopia, rather than the play imitating an existing reality. That utopia is a place built out of those moments when all hierarchies are reversed as a prelude to revolution. So the butler begins the play with subversive witticisms which excel those of his master, and the master thereafter goes in search of his half-suppressed double.

The psychologist Otto Rank has argued that the double, being a handy device for the offloading of all that embarrasses, may epitomize one's noble soul or one's base guilts, or indeed both at the same time. That is to say that the double is a close relation of the Englishman's Celtic Other. Many characters in literature have sought to murder their double in order to do away with guilt (as England had tried to annihilate Irish culture), but have then found that it is not so easily repressed, since it may also contain man's utopian self (those redemptive qualities found by Arnold in Ireland). Bunbury is Algy's double, embodying in a single fiction all that is most creative and most corrupt in his creator. Bunbury is the shadow which symbolizes Algy's need for immortality, for an influential soul that survives death; and, at the same time, Bunbury is that ignoble being to whom the irresponsible Algy transfers all responsibility for his more questionable deeds. The service which the Irish performed for the English, Bunbury discharges for his creator: he epitomizes his master's need for a human likeness on the planet and, simultaneously, his desire to retain his own difference. Hence the play is one long debate about whether or not to do away with Bunbury. Lady Bracknell's complaints sound suspiciously like English claims that, in trying to solve the Irish Question, the Irish kept on changing it: 'I think it is high time that Mr Bunbury made up his mind whether he was going to live or to die. This shilly-shallying with the question is absurd. Nor do I in any way approve of the modern sympathy with invalids. I consider it morbid.'

[Psychologist] Erich Stern has written that 'in order to escape the fear of death, the person resorts to suicide which, however, he carries out on his double because he loves and esteems his ego so much'. Many analysts would contend that the double is the creation of a pathologically self-absorbed type, usually male, often chauvinistic, sometimes imperialist: only by this device of splitting can such a one live with himself. Rank actually argued that the double arose from a morbid self-love which prevented the development of a balanced personality. If this is so, however, then killing or annihilating the double is no final solution, for his life and welfare are as closely linked to that of his author as are the Irish to the English, women to men, and so on. No sooner is the double denied than it becomes man's fate. Like the 'Celtic feminine' in a culture of imperial machismo, it comes back to haunt its begetters, enacting what Wilde called the tyranny of the weak over the strong, the only kind of tyranny which lasts. So, in the play, whenever he is most stridently denied, the double always turns out to be closest at hand. When Jack exclaims, 'My brother is in the dining-room? I don't know what it all means. I think it is perfectly absurd,' Algy asks, perhaps on behalf of all uninvited Irish guests: 'Why on earth don't you go up and change? . . . It is perfectly childish to be in deep mourning for a man who is actually staying for a whole week with you in your house as a guest. I call it grotesque.' The denied double thus ends up setting the agenda of its creator, who, being unaware of it, becomes its unconscious slave. The women in the play set the agenda for men, Bunbury for Algy, butlers for masters, and so on, even as the Irish Parnellites [followers of Thomas Parnell, Irish poet and clergyman] were setting the agenda for England, repeatedly paralysing politics at Westminster.

Writers throughout history have found their version of the double in art, that diabolical enterprise which paradoxically guarantees immortality; and this is the one employment of the double which may not be a form of neurosis, since it is presented 'in an acceptable form, justifying the survival of the irrational in our over-rational civilization'. But other uses are pathological and doomed, since the double is devised to cope with the fear of death but reappears as its very portent. That fear gives rise to an exaggerated attitude to one's own ego, leading to an inability to love and a wild longing to be loved. These, sure enough, are attributes of Algy and Jack before the women break up their self-enclosed rituals (and, it might be added, attributes of British policy in Ireland before independence).

There could hardly be a more convincing psychological explanation of the strange oscillation between conciliation and coercion in imperial policy towards Ireland than Rank's report on the tactics employed in the making of the double.

The notion of the 'innocent' and 'spontaneous' Irish may have been an emotional convenience to those Victorians who were increasingly unable to find satisfaction for feelings of guilt in universally accepted religious forms. The myth of an unspoilt peasantry, in Cumberland or Connemara, was, after all, a convenient means of emotional absolution from guilt in a society for which natural instinct was often tantamount to a vice. The sequence of coercion following upon conciliation could be explained in terms of outrage with the symbol when it failed to live up to these high expectations.

If this is so, then *The Importance of Being Earnest* becomes (among other things, of course) a parable of Anglo-Irish relations and a pointer to their resolution. This should not seem surprising. Wilde, in London, offering witty critiques of imperial culture, was one of the first in a long line of native intellectuals who were equipped by an analytic education to pen the most thorough repudiation of their masters.

The Philosophy of the Dandy

Arthur Ganz

Arthur Ganz argues that dandyism is Wilde's philosophy and attitude toward life. This philosophy stems from Wilde's rejection of the middle-class society of his day, which he considered coarse and pitiless. For Wilde the dandy is an individual who uses wit to express his superiority over the ordinary and crass world around him.

According to Ganz, Wilde sees the dandy as a subversive who trivializes social institutions as a way to safely mock them. For example, middle-class morality in *The Importance of Being Earnest* is made to appear ridiculous. Ganz writes further that in Wilde's philosophy the dandy is intensely individualistic, absorbed entirely in his own feelings. Indeed, the dandy is even reluctant to admit the existence or emotional needs of others. This allows the dandy to reject or abuse others as he pleases; no exterior force can affect the dandy's personality. For the dandy, all values come from self; hence, the moral standards of others are irrelevant.

Arthur Ganz teaches English at Rutgers University, New Brunswick, New Jersey. He has contributed to many literary periodicals and is the coauthor of *A Reader's Guide to Literary Terms*.

In act II of *The Importance of Being Earnest* Jack returns to his country house and announces the death of his supposed brother, the profligate Ernest.

DR. CHASUBLE: Was the cause of death mentioned?

JACK: A severe chill, it seems.

MISS PRISM: As a man sows, so shall he reap.

DR. CHASUBLE: (Raising his hand) Charity, dear Miss Prism, charity! None of us is perfect. I myself am peculiarly susceptible to draughts.

Excerpted from "The Meaning of *The Importance of Being Earnest*," by Arthur Ganz, *Modern Drama*, vol. 6, 1963. Reprinted with permission from *Modern Drama*.

This sequence is more than a delightful joke. It is symptomatic of the emotional and intellectual attitudes that underlie the play and, in fact, Wilde's work. What we laugh at, perhaps a little uneasily, is Chasuble's inability to distinguish between a moral and a physical quality. When the rector cautions Miss Prism about the inevitable imperfections of man and goes on to name one of his own, we naturally expect a moral failing, but we get instead a susceptibility to draughts. If we are uneasy, it is because in the world in which Dr. Chasuble exists, the world of perfect Wildean dandyism, the rector's attitude is entirely reasonable. This is a world of pure form, and the distinction between a moral and a physical failing, between external and internal, does not exist. Chasuble is right and we are wrong.

Even such a brief analysis of one line suggests that the conventional description of *The Importance* as, in the words of [critic] Arthur Symons, "a sort of sublime farce, meaningless and delightful," is inadequate. [Critic] William Archer was so puzzled by the play that he asked, "What can a poor critic do with a play which raises no principle, whether of art or morals . . . and is nothing but an absolutely wilful expression of an irrepressibly witty personality?" With the advantage of distance, we can see now that art and morals are precisely the subjects of *The Importance of Being Earnest* and that the world of dandyism, though delightful, is far from meaningless.

DANDYISM AS AN ATTITUDE TOWARD LIFE

For Wilde, dandyism was a philosophy and an attitude toward life. Embodied in his plays, it functions as a rationale for the actions and attitudes of his characters, as a coherent system which forms the basis for their thoughts and their conduct. In the great tradition of the Romantic exile artist, Wilde rejected the middle-class, Philistine society of his day. Its coarseness, its pitiless morality, and its incomprehension of beauty were all alien to him. Searching for a new basis for life, Wilde, the most extreme of esthetic critics, turned to the only part of experience in which he had faith, to art—whose secret for him lay always in the achievement of perfect form. He took form, the basis of art, turned it into a philosophy of life in which esthetics replaces ethics and, as we shall see, introduced it into his plays cloaked with the elegance and wit of nineteenth-century dandyism.

This dandyism, from which Wilde drew so many elements sympathetic to him, had existed long before he made use of it. The nineteenth century produced many dandies, and Wilde must have seen himself as a follower of such men as Brummell, Byron, d'Orsay, and, probably above all others, [English statesman and novelist] Benjamin Disraeli. In Disraeli, Wilde saw an artist like himself, a man apart from the crass bourgeosie, whose wit and extraordinary dress were instruments with which he had achieved a position of power. With Disraeli in mind, a remark by Lord Illingworth in *A Woman of No Importance,* "a man who can dominate a London dinner table can dominate the world," is a little less bizarre than it at first seems.

Disraeli, however, was only an example. The theorists of dandyism as a philosophy of life and art were [French philosopher] Jules Barbey d'Aurevilly and [French poet] Charles Baudelaire. Barbey d'Aurevilly, still a figure of some note when Wilde frequented Parisian literary circles, had produced *Du Dandysme et de Georges Brummell,* the most elaborate nineteenth-century disquisition on dandyism. Barbey never saw dandyism as a mere matter of elegance in dress, but as a philosophy, as a "manner of living composed entirely of nuance, as always happens in societies at once very ancient and very civilized." His insistence on dandyism as a rule of conduct for a society past its prime must have impressed the decadents of the nineties, but the element which would most have appealed to Wilde was Barbey's view of the dandy as individualist, as "the element of caprice in a stratified and symmetrical society." The dandy demonstrates his individualism and superiority with his wit, by shocking without being shocked. He is one of those "who wish to produce surprise while remaining impassive."

If Wilde did not learn the theory of dandyism from Barbey, he undoubtedly learned, or at any rate reinforced, it through the essay "Le Dandy" in *Le peintre de la vie moderne* by Charles Baudelaire. Wilde admired Baudelaire and could not have been unfamiliar with an essay by him on a subject so important in Wilde's own work. Like Barbey, Baudelaire insisted that "dandyism is not, as many unreflecting persons seem to think, an immoderate taste for dress and material elegance. These things are for the perfect dandy only a symbol of the aristocratic superiority of his spirit." Dandyism is individualism, "the ardent need to produce something original . . . it is a kind of cult of the self . . . it is the pleasure of astonishing and the proud satisfaction of never being astonished." The dandy is hostile to his society, for only in an effete and unworthy age would he feel this compulsion to distinguish himself from the ordinary. "Dandyism," wrote Baudelaire, "is the last burst of heroism in a decadent age." Wilde called dandyism a philosophy; Baudelaire went even further: "in fact," he wrote, "I would not be entirely wrong in considering dandyism as a sort of religion.

THE DANDY AS A SUBVERSIVE

Now we can turn to Wilde's plays and see what led him to make the religion of dandyism his personal code, what he took from his sources, and what he added to them. To Wilde, as to Barbey d'Aurevilly and Baudelaire, dandyism was not an affectation of dress but an attitude toward the world, and specifically toward the world of Victorian Philistinism with its coarseness, its materialism, and its code of Puritanical morality. The French theorists reinforced in Wilde the idea of the dandy as a heroic individualist who, like Disraeli as Wilde saw him, used his grace and wit to oppose and dominate the crass world about him. It is of the essence of *The Importance of Being Earnest*, however, that this Philistine world, though often spoken of, is never present. If it were, the play as we know it could not exist. Wilde's society comedies, in which the Philistine world has equal status with the dandiacal, are disfigured by the conflict between them. In each play a similar pattern of melodramatic action is centered around a character with a secret sin in his past: Mrs. Erlynne, Mrs. Arbuthnot, Sir Robert Chiltern. Each is opposed by a strict Puritan—Lady Windermere, Hester Worsley, Lady Chiltern—who at first allows of no compromise between good and bad and demands that sin be punished. In each case, however, the sinner is shown to have remained pure at heart and to desire forgiveness while the Puritan is educated to grant it and even to come to love him. Like the dandy, the sinner is an exile, but one who cannot bear his solitude and begs to be forgiven and accepted by the ordinary Philistine world. The dandy, however, glories in his alienation. It is the uncomfortable yoking of these antithetical attitudes that finally destroys the society comedies. To write his masterpiece, Wilde had to reject the passionate sinner with his admission of guilt and speak only in the critical voice of the dandy.

But dandiacal criticism should be distinguished from satire, for when the dandy is satirical at all, he is so only incidentally. Wilde can satirize such things as the methodical husband hunting of fashionable society, as when Lady Bracknell tells Jack that he is not down on her list of eligible young men, "although," she says, "I have the same list as the dear Duchess of Bolton has. We work together, in fact." In this case, Wilde agrees with the ostensible opinion of society, that arranged, mercenary marriages are evil. This agreement, rare in Wilde, is essential to the satirist who accepts a social norm and criticizes deviations from it, but the dandy is himself a deviation and criticizes the social norm. Dandyism, as Baudelaire and Barbey maintained, is hostile to ordinary society. The dandy is not a reformer but a subversive.

To call such a dandy as the charming and witty Algernon a subversive may seem at first unduly harsh. Algernon, one might say, is only trivial. But triviality is the dandy's disguise. It is, in fact, the traditional clown's mask, from the concealment of which he can say what he wishes without fear of retaliation. In Wilde's other plays the dandies are often openly villainous, but here, through the unreality of the situations and the delicacy of the language, Wilde has thrown a cloak of seeming innocence over a very sinister personage. Algernon's statements, then, may be flippant in tone, but they are not innocuous in content. Where the satirist makes fun of the abuses of marriage, the dandy criticizes the institution itself. When the manservant Lane observes that in married households the champagne is rarely of a first-rate brand, Algernon exclaims, "Good Heavens! Is marriage so demoralizing as that?" He tries to avoid Lady Bracknell's dinner party because he knows he will be placed "next to Mary Farquhar, who always flirts with her own husband across the dinner table. That is not very pleasant. Indeed, it is not even decent." Lady Bracknell herself, though she is an arch-Philistine, often assumes the dandiacal voice and shares Algernon's point of view. "I'm sorry if we are a little late, Algernon," she says upon entering, "but I was obliged to call upon dear Lady Harbury. I hadn't seen her since her poor husband's death. I never saw a woman so altered; she looks quite twenty years younger." In the third act she makes herself even clearer. Commenting on Jack's father, she remarks that he was eccentric, "but only in later years. And that was the result of the Indian climate, and marriage, and indigestion, and other things of that kind." Like Dr. Chasuble, she cannot distinguish between the physical and the spiritual, between indigestion and a sacrament of the church.

THE DANDY AND MIDDLE-CLASS MORALITY

Lady Bracknell and Dr. Chasuble are dandies by indirection; just as they conceal their dandyism beneath a Philistine exterior, so Jack, seemingly virtuous and respectable, is as belligerent as they are. Several times during the play he refers to truth, a quality admired by all righteous men, but when Algernon asks him if he intends to tell Gwendolen the truth about being Ernest in town and Jack in the country, Jack replies patronizingly, "My dear fellow, the truth isn't quite the sort of thing one tells to a nice, sweet, refined girl." Later, when forced to admit his deception, he says, "Gwendolen—Cecily—it is very painful for me to be forced to speak the truth. It is the first time in my life that I have ever been reduced to such a painful position, and I am really quite inexperienced in doing anything of the kind." When it is finally revealed that Jack's name really is Ernest, he can only exclaim, "Gwendolen, it is a terrible thing for a man to find out suddenly that all his life he has been speaking nothing but the truth. Can you forgive me?"

Even the ingenuous Cecily turns out to be a foe of rectitude and morality. "Dear Uncle Jack is so very serious," she remarks. "Sometimes he is so serious that I think he cannot be quite well." When Gwendolen is announced, Cecily at first supposes her to be an elderly lady interested in philanthropic work. "I don't quite like women who are interested in philanthropic work," she says to herself. "I think it so forward of them." Cecily shares this distaste with Lady Bracknell who, misunderstanding Algernon's statement that Bunbury had been quite exploded, cries, "Exploded! Was he the victim of a revolutionary outrage? I was not aware that Mr. Bunbury was interested in social legislation. If so, he is well punished for his morbidity."

It is, in fact, the arch-Philistine Lady Bracknell who, when speaking in her dandiacal voice, most openly defies the Philistine standards:

LADY BRACKNELL: Is this Miss Prism a female of repellent aspect, remotely connected with education?

CHASUBLE: (Somewhat indignantly) She is the most cultivated of ladies, and the very picture of respectability.

LADY BRACKNELL: It is obviously the same person.

It is unnecessary to continue adding examples. Whenever ordinary morality appears, it is made to seem ridiculous. Even Miss Prism becomes an unintentional exponent of the dandiacal attitude. When it is announced that the carefree Ernest is dead, she exclaims, "What a lesson for him! I trust he will profit by it." When we laugh at her obtuseness, we are forced to laugh at even the possibility of moral reform.

THE DANDY AND INDIVIDUALISM

Miss Prism also illustrates another significant element in the play, the intense individualism that was one of Wilde's major preoccupations. Absorbed in the contemplation of his own feelings, the dandiacal individualist seems reluctant to admit the existence of others, or at least to react to their emotions. When, for example, Jack rushes in with the crucial handbag and begs Miss Prism to identify it and thus establish his parentage, she examines it carefully and at considerable length:

> MISS PRISM: And here on the lock are my initials. I had forgotten that in an extravagant mood I had had them placed there. The bag is undoubtedly mine. I am delighted to have it so unexpectedly restored to me. It has been a great inconvenience being without it all these years.

At this climactic moment of the play when the secret of Jack's birth is about to be penetrated, Miss Prism's mind is centered on a minor personal acquisition.

Although our laughter at the incongruousness of her remark conceals its inhumanity, there is in Miss Prism's foolish preoccupation with her handbag something similar to the icy self-sufficiency of Gwendolen and Cecily, both of whom happily center their affections on the name Ernest before they come to know its possessor. Cecily, in fact, manages to conduct an elaborate courtship in the absence of her beloved. Lady Bracknell is not only an individualist in her self-sufficiency but in what she implies about keeping the personality inviolate. When Jack hurries upstairs to hunt frantically for the handbag, she remarks, "This noise is extremely unpleasant. It sounds as if he was having an argument. I dislike arguments of any kind. They are always vulgar and often convincing." Beneath this joke is Wilde's reluctance to let any exterior force affect his personality. He was engrossed in what Baudelaire called "the cult of the self." Even in prison Wilde wrote, "I am far more of an individualist than I ever was. Nothing seems to me of the smallest value except what one gets out of oneself. My nature is seeking a fresh mode of self-realization. That is all I am concerned with."

THE DANDY'S SELF-CENTERED FOCUS ON SENSATION

The dandy's individualism is closely connected with his social belligerence. By taking the limits of his own personality as the boundaries of admissible reality, he can protect himself against the claims of society. If all values come from the self, then the moral standards of others are irrelevant to him; he may abuse or disregard them as he pleases. For him other persons have little real existence; they are only one of the mediums through which sensations, pleasant or otherwise, are conveyed to him. But the sensations themselves are important, for it is through them that the dandy creates the self. The theory of sensation came to Wilde from Walter Pater, his master at Oxford, whose famous conclusion to *The Renaissance* emphasized "not the fruit of experience, but experience itself." To the dandy, remote from society and centered on himself, his own feelings are matters of extraordinary interest. The more exquisite sensations he can experience, the richer will be the self which he is trying to realize.

It is this desire to savor a novel experience that makes Algernon, when returning Jack's cigarette case and asking his friend to explain why he is Ernest in town and Jack in the country, say, as he hands Jack the case, "Here it is. Now produce your explanation, and pray make it improbable." However, the characters most given to relishing new sensations are Cecily and Gwendolen. While awaiting the entrance of the reprobate Ernest, impersonated by Algernon, Cecily remarks, "I have never met any really wicked person before. I feel rather frightened. I am so afraid he will look just like everyone else." And when Algernon enters, "very gay and debonair," she sighs in disappointment, "he does!" Cecily does not fear Ernest's wickedness; she fears that if he does not *seem* wicked, he will fail to give her the *nouveau frisson* that she seeks. Later, when Algernon-Ernest says that their parting will be very painful, Cecily replies, "It is always painful to part from people whom one has known for a very brief space of time. The absence of old friends one can endure with equanimity. But even a momentary separation from anyone to whom one has just been introduced is almost unbearable." A new acquaintance is a "new thrill." It is the loss of the sensation, not the friend, that Cecily fears. Perhaps the clearest illustration of the dandy's self-centered relishing of sensation is the line Gwendolen speaks while Jack is upstairs frantically hunting for the handbag that will reveal his identity. "This suspense is terrible," she exclaims; "I hope it will last." The continuation of Gwendolen's pleasurable sensation is dependent upon the continuation of Jack's distress, but such a consideration cannot affect her. Locked within the confines of the individual self, the dandy must feed upon a succession of novelties or starve to death.

THE DANDY AND AESTHETICS

Although the stress on sensation was added by Wilde to the belligerence and individualism inherited from Barbey and Baudelaire, it is not the Wildean dandy's most distinctive element. This is his faith in the superiority of aesthetic form. "In matters of grave importance," says Gwendolen, "style not sincerity is the vital thing." Baudelaire also stressed the superiority of the artificial to the natural and admired the conscious artifice of the dandy's toilette, but he emphasized the dandy's revulsion from the moral standards of his age and only by implication connected him with aesthetics. For Wilde, the dandy embodied, above all, his theories of art. When Wilde wrote that Phipps, the dandiacal butler of *An Ideal Husband,* "represents the dominance of form," he made the dandy the incarnation of aesthetic form; and for Wilde form, as he explained in "The Critic as Artist," was the basis of all art:

> For the real artist is he who proceeds, not from feeling to form, but from form to thought and passion . . . realizing the beauty of the sonnet-scheme, he conceives certain modes of music and methods of rhyme, and the mere form suggests what is to fill it and make it intellectually and emotionally complete. . . . He gains his inspiration from form, and from form purely, as an artist should. . . . In every sphere of life Form is the beginning of things. The rhythmic harmonious gestures of dancing convey, Plato tells us, both rhythm and harmony into the mind. . . . Yes, Form is everything. It is the secret of life.

It is this element, this absolute faith in pure aesthetic form, that makes the Wildean dandy unique, and because it is dominated by him *The Importance of Being Earnest* is a unique play. It stands alone among English comedies, not only because of the quality of its wit, but because it is an expression of Wilde's theories and attitudes, and no other writer has approached the theater with a comparable point of view. It stands alone among Wilde's plays because the dandiacal element in *The Importance,* unlike that in the society comedies, is not in open conflict with a Philistine element and limited to its own sections of the play but appears everywhere and makes of the entire work a kind of dandiacal Utopia, a world of perfect form. "For the canons of good society," Wilde wrote in *Dorian Gray,* "are, or should be, the same as the canons of art. Form is absolutely essential to it."

Form for Wilde is found only in art, never in nature. It is in speaking of nature that the dandy's preference for the artificial is most clearly revealed. During the interview scene in Act I, Lady Bracknell expresses her disapproval of Jack's house in the country. "A country house!" she exclaims, ". . . You have a town house, I hope? A girl with a simple, unspoiled nature, like Gwendolen, could hardly be expected to reside in the country." The opening pages of "The Decay of Lying" offer a particularly clear gloss on this speech. "My own experience," says Vivian, the elegant purveyor of dandiacal opinions, "is that the more we study Art, the less we care for Nature. What Art really reveals to us is Nature's lack of design, her curious crudities . . . her absolutely unfinished condition. . . . Art is our spirited protest, our gallant attempt to teach Nature her proper place." Lady Bracknell takes the same attitude toward Cecily's lack of artificial elegance:

> LADY BRACKNELL: . . . Pretty child! Your dress is sadly simple, and your hair seems almost as nature might have left it. But we can soon alter all that. A thoroughly experienced French maid produces a really marvelous effect in a very brief space of time.

It is always perfection of form that the dandy seeks; content is irrelevant to him. After one of Algernon's more outrageous sallies, Jack exclaims in exasperation, "Is that clever?" Algernon replies, "It is perfectly phrased! and quite as true as any observation in civilized life should be." Even Algernon's servant, Lane, is revealed as a dandy. When Algernon remarks, "Lane, you're a perfect pessimist," the manservant replies, "I do my best to give satisfaction, sir." For the dandy, to be recognized as having achieved perfection in anything is the highest accolade.

This insistence on perfect aesthetic form has many disguises, as, for example, when Gwendolen asks, "Cecily, mamma, whose views on education are remarkably strict, has brought me up to be extremely short-sighted; it is part of her system; so do you mind my looking at you through my glasses?" The fact that Gwendolen may have twenty-twenty vision is irrelevant if propriety demands that she be short-sighted. She is a conscious, artistic creation and must obey the rules of form.

Often, however, the dandy speaks without any disguise, and no one is more open than the seemingly innocent Cecily. When Algernon says that he has pretended to be Ernest in order to meet her, she asks Gwendolen's opinion of this excuse:

CECILY: (To Gwendolen) That certainly seems a satisfactory explanation, does it not?

GWENDOLEN: Yes, dear, if you can believe him.

CECILY: I don't. But that does not affect the wonderful beauty of his answer.

The dandy, with his code of artistic form, is indifferent to both Philistine truth and Philistine morality. When Algernon admires a trinket which Cecily has given herself on his behalf, she remarks, "Yes, you've wonderfully good taste, Ernest. It's the excuse I've always given for your leading such a bad life." This obliteration of conventional morality is nowhere so apparent as in Cecily's first words to the disguised Algernon:

CECILY:You, I see from your card, are Uncle Jack's brother, my cousin Ernest, my wicked cousin Ernest.

ALGERNON: Oh! I am not really wicked at all, cousin Cecily. You mustn't think that I am wicked.

CECILY: If you are not, then you have certainly been deceiving us all in a very inexcusable manner. I hope you have not been leading a double life, pretending to be wicked and being really good all the time. That would be hypocrisy.

In the dandiacal system moral standards do not exist, although the terminology of morality is sometimes used. The dandy is concerned only with propriety; for him the proper course of conduct for a wicked brother is to be wicked. Goodness would be indecorous and the pretense of wickedness hypocritical. But since dandiacal wickedness is only a particular mode of achieving beauty, evil cannot exist in the dandy's world, and Cecily has no more sense of it than Dr. Chasuble, who cannot distinguish between a moral flaw and a susceptibility to draughts.

In one form or another dandyism dominates *The Importance of Being Earnest.* Even the pun in its title conceals a dandiacal meaning. As the various couples embrace at the end of the play, Lady Bracknell rebukes her new-found nephew:

> LADY BRACKNELL: My nephew, you seem to be displaying signs of triviality.
>
> JACK: On the contrary, Aunt Augusta, I've now realized for the first time in my life the vital Importance of Being Earnest.

When Lady Bracknell accuses Jack of being trivial, he replies that he realizes the importance of being earnest, or sincere and moral, but lurking beneath the reassuring, Philistine earnest is the dandiacal Ernest, for the name Ernest is a beautiful form which the self-centered, dandiacal heroines love while remaining indifferent to its content, the character of its bearer. To realize the importance of being Ernest is to understand the dominance of form; it is to be a Wildean dandy. The graceful pun that seems to set a tone of careless humor epitomizes in itself the meaning that can be found on almost every page of Wilde's masterpiece.

Wilde's Vision of Nothingness

David Parker

David Parker argues that *The Importance of Being Earnest* addresses the issue of human identity. The playwright contemplates nothingness, or the notion that identity is insubstantial and the structures and norms of society trifling. In particular, conventional attitudes toward the family are broken down in the play. The family is transformed so that the characters believe they can invent brothers, mothers, and ideal husbands. According to Parker, in Wilde's vision of nothingness, identity dissolves. Each character achieves identity through personal acts of imagination. In a mutable, insubstantial world, relationships, like the one between Gwendolen and Cecily, change dramatically on whim and impulse. Parker explains that love, like identity, is an impulse without substance, and that Wilde sees love as a creative act that is subject to fantasy and wit.

In the world of the play, truth is a collection of separate, deceptive, and contradictory impressions. Parker maintains that Wilde depicts truth as insignificant, something that cannot be discovered through the intellect. The male characters rely on deception and posturing and the female characters impose pleasing but untrue fantasies on the world.

David Parker is a professor of English at the University of Malaya. He contributes articles to numerous literary periodicals.

Wilde consciously exploits the concern of farce with human identity. The joke in the title is often thought of as a mock-pompous piece of frivolity, but it is more than that. The play might as justly be named "The Importance of Being." The

Excerpted from "Oscar Wilde's Great Farce: *The Importance of Being Earnest*," by David Parker, *Modern Language Quarterly*, vol. 35, no. 2, June 1974. Copyright © 1974 by the University of Washington. Reprinted with permission from Duke University Press.

whole thing is comically addressed to the problem of recognizing and defining human identity; we are made to see wide significance in Jack's polite request, "Lady Bracknell, I hate to seem inquisitive, but would you kindly inform me who I am?" The pun on *earnest* and *Ernest* merely makes the title more suitably comic. Neither being earnest nor being Ernest is of much help when confidence is lost in the substantiality of human identity. The concern with identity is repeatedly underlined in the text of the play, where statements that seem superficially only to poke fun at upper-class frivolity continually edge the mind toward a contemplation of the insubstantiality of identity. "It isn't easy to be anything nowadays," complains Algy in the first act. "There's such a lot of beastly competition about." And only a few lines later, Gwendolen feels obliged to deny that she is perfect: "It would leave no room for developments, and I intend to develop in many directions."

More than most writers of farce, Wilde was conscious of this concern with identity, so natural to the form, and he uses it to express a preoccupation which the nineteenth century gave birth to, and the twentieth century cherishes. Lurking always in the depths of the play is a steady contemplation of Nothingness, of *le néant*, which is all the more effective for its being, in contrast to most of its manifestations, comic in mode. Instead of making Nothingness a pretext for despair, Wilde finds in it a challenge to the imagination. For him, Nothingness in human identity, in human claims to knowledge, in the organization of society, becomes a field to be tilled by the artist—by the artist in each of us. . . .

WILDE CHALLENGES CONVENTIONAL NOTIONS ABOUT FAMILY LIFE

Wilde depicts a world in which the socially endorsed certainties are continually evaporating; values respecting social class, education, the Church, money, love, and the family undergo constant metamorphosis. Attitudes toward the family, in particular, are grotesquely transformed. Algy cheerfully dismisses the sentiments associated with kinship: "Relations are simply a tedious pack of tedious people, who haven't got the remotest knowledge of how to live, nor the smallest instinct about when to die." Others invert the normal sentiments. Lady Bracknell speaks of an acquaintance whose husband has died: "I never saw a woman so altered, she looks quite twenty years younger." Gwendolen complains about her lack of influence over her mother: "Few parents nowadays pay any regard to what their children say to them! The old-fashioned respect for the young is rapidly dying out." She approves of her father's domestication, however: "The home seems to me to be the proper sphere for the man. And certainly once a man begins to neglect his domestic duties he becomes painfully effeminate, does he not?"

In plot and action, too, conventional notions about family life are broken down. The handbag in Jack's family history excites Lady Bracknell's famous protest: "To be born, or at any rate bred in a handbag, whether it had handles or not, seems to me to display a contempt for the ordinary decencies of family life that reminds one of the worst excesses of the French Revolution." The comedy is enhanced, of course, by the oddity of Lady Bracknell's own notions (or at least her way of expressing them). She seems to conceive family as something subject to human volition, and can advise Jack "to make a definite effort to produce, at any rate, one parent, of either sex, before the season is quite over." Though we may see parody of upper-class snobbery here, others do will relations into—and out of—existence, without there being any feeling of parody. Jack invents a brother; the girls invent ideal husbands. (Algy's Bunbury is only a friend, but the effect is much the same.) At the other extreme, the characters accept the family relationships revealed at the end of the play, with an absurd eagerness that is just as effective in ridiculing conventional notions. This is particularly evident in Jack's outburst, when he mistakenly assumes Miss Prism to be his mother. She indignantly reminds him that she is unmarried. "Cannot repentance wipe out an act of folly?" he cries. "Why should there be one law for men and another for women? Mother! I forgive you." The family is a category of everyday understanding that is one of the first to crumble before the vision of Nothingness. That is what enables Wilde's characters to adopt such a variety of postures with respect to it.

WILDE CHALLENGES CONVENTIONAL NOTIONS OF IDENTITY

Individual identity, too, dissolves before the vision of Nothingness. That is why farce, and its traditional concern with human identity, was so useful to Wilde. Each character in *The Importance of Being Earnest* is a sort of vacuum that attains to individual identity only through an effort of the creative imagination. They are like [French philosopher and dramatist Jean-Paul] Sartre's famous waiter in *L'Être et le Néant,* except that they make their decisions consciously, and that we are pleased rather than nauseated by the process. Each attains to identity in the mode of *being what he is not.*

It is a sense of the insubstantiality of human identity which causes Wilde to place such emphasis on impulse (on selfishness, if you like). Admit all the problems of epistemology, and impulse still remains. Obedience to impulse is a defiant way of asserting some sort of basic identity. Algy's obsession with food is an example. "I hate people who are not serious about meals," he complains. "It is so shallow of them." Beneath the parody of manners, we can detect in this a perception, truthful within the terms of reference the play allows. Algy is prepared to use the word *serious* here because there is something fundamental to relate it to. When appetites are all that is substantial in human identity, all else must seem shallow. The two girls place a similar reliance on impulse. Both have faith in first impressions, and both are surprisingly candid about their sexual appetites. Cecily tells Algy, "I don't think you should tell me that you love me wildly, passionately, devotedly, hopelessly. Hopelessly doesn't seem to make much sense, does it?"

They are quick to change, though. When, after mutual declarations of devotion, Algy tells Cecily he will wait seventeen years for her hand, she replies, "Yes, I felt it instinctively. And I am so sorry for you, Algy. Because I couldn't wait all that time. I hate waiting even five minutes for anybody. It always makes me rather cross. I am not punctual myself, I know, but I do like punctuality in others, and waiting even to be married is quite out of the question." Changeability, in fact, is a corollary of obedience to impulse. As impulses vary, so must the attitudes of the individual. The protagonists of Wilde's play recognize this, particularly the girls. "I never change, except in my affections," Gwendolen announces. Their changeability is most amusingly demonstrated in the first meeting of Gwendolen and Cecily, when, in the course of a single scene, they proceed from mutual suspicion to mutual affection, thence to mutual detestation, and finally to mutual affection again, all the time firmly maintaining that they are consistent. The audience is likely to laugh at this sort of thing because it realizes that literary and social conventions are being ridiculed, but there is more to the comedy than that. There is a core of truth in what we are presented with: human beings do change. The joke lies in the way the characters are neither distressed nor surprised at their own changeability. In Wilde's world nothing else is expected.

LOVE AS IMPULSE, FANTASY, AND WIT

Love might seem a surprising ingredient in such a world, but it is a play of courtship, and love does have importance in it. Love is based on impulse, after all, and for Wilde it is action, not object; a courageous creative effort of the will, not a substantial inner something; the free play of the imagination, not a faculty. The characters of the play constantly deny the substantiality of love, in speech and action. Their courtships consist in patterns of interlocking fantasy and wit; they woo through imposture and fancy; they pursue and fly; they test and torment each other. Never is there anything static or certain about their relationships. "The very essence of romance is uncertainty," says Algy. "If ever I get married, I'll certainly try to forget the fact." Wilde is following Restoration comedy again, here. "Uncertainty and Expectation are the joys of Life," says [English dramatist William] Congreve's Angelica. "Security is an insipid thing, and the overtaking and possessing of a Wish, discovers the Folly of the Chase." And as with Restoration comedy, we admire the lovers for their courage and their wit. We feel that they are absurd too (all action in the play is absurd; the secret is not minding), but at the same time we are made to feel that they are somehow right as well. The theme of sentimental education, normally found in romantic comedy, is parodied by inversion. Fantasies the lovers have about each other are confirmed rather than cured, almost as if wit, the creative imagination (call it what you will), were able magically to force the world into the shapes it suggests to itself. We feel, at any rate, that the lovers earn their partners by growing toward them, through wit.

THE INSIGNIFICANCE OF TRUTH

Because the characters live in a world in which order is constantly vanishing, they scorn theory, consistency, and the appearance of simplicity. "The truth," as Algy says, "is rarely pure and never simple." Certainly, in matters of identity, seeming intelligibility is to be distrusted. "The simplicity of your nature," Gwendolen tells Jack, "makes you exquisitely incomprehensible to me." The characters are alert, not to a harmonious universal nature, but to a proliferation of separate, deceptive, and contradictory sense-impressions. Knowledge comes only through the imagination. Gwendolen laughs at Jack's misgivings over her delight in his being called (as she thinks) Ernest. He cautiously inquires how she might feel were his name not Ernest, but she will not listen. "Ah, that is clearly a metaphysical speculation," she says, "and like all metaphysical speculation, has very little reference at all to the actual facts of real life, as we know them." This is an ironic node. The observation by itself fits in with the general theme of the play, but in the immediate context the joke is against Gwendolen (and Jack, when we think how he must feel). He has only assumed the name of Ernest; her notions are just as "metaphysical"; and what seem to be the actual facts of real life thoroughly justify such a speculation. Yet at the end of the play, Gwendolen's faith in the name, her conviction that she will marry an Ernest, and her insistence that her lover conform to her ideal are all justified; we learn that Jack's true name is Ernest. One effect of all this is to satirize faith in ideals by having it vindicated absurdly, but there is more to it than that. We feel delighted at the outcome, not like the recipients of a warning. We are made to feel that confident fantasies justify themselves, that a bold imagination is more useful than plodding attention to apparent facts.

In Wilde's world truth itself dwindles into insignificance. The characters have a strictly practical attitude to the relationship between statements and actuality, the latter being so elusive. Charged with being named John, Jack declares, "I could deny it if I liked. I could deny anything if I liked." And he is embarrassed when required to utter things in strict correspondence with what seem to be facts: "it is very painful for me to be forced to speak the truth. It is the first time in my life that I have ever been reduced to such a painful position, and I am really quite inexperienced in doing anything of the kind, so you must excuse me if I stammer in my tale." He goes on to say that he has never had a brother, which turns out to be untrue; Algy is his brother. Once again the inference is that truth cannot be discovered through the senses and the intellect alone. Jack's witty lies are more percipient [discerning]. The comic inversion of truth and untruth is maintained in Jack's dismay, when he learns that what he had thought to be lies are true. "Gwendolen," he says, "it is a terrible thing for a man to find out suddenly that all his life he has been speaking nothing but the truth. Can you forgive me?" She can. "There is always hope," she says. "even for those who are most accurate in their statements." Even when it is the art of living, we are tempted to gloss, "Lying, the telling of beautiful untrue things, is the proper aim of Art."

FANTASIES OF THE CHARACTERS

Jack and Algy certainly attain their ends through lying. They are true rogues, impulsive, lovers of deception and imposture. They fulfill themselves in the way of all rogues: by discovering human freedom in protean identity. Doubtless what they do permits us to laugh at the mad antics young gentlemen get up to, even to disapprove mildly, but the candid spectator will admit that their tricks inspire above all else a feeling of moral liberation. Jack's double life may be exposed, Algy's Bunbury may be deprived of his existence, but these deceptions serve their purpose, and part of us at least is glad.

Gwendolen and Cecily rely on beautiful untrue things as much as their suitors do, but instead of deceiving the world through imposture, they demand that the world accept the pleasing fantasies they choose to project onto it. The heroes adopt identities to suit the occasion; the heroines imagine identities to suit the persons with whom they choose to associate. Gwendolen explains her principles in love: "We live, as I hope you know, Mr Worthing, in an age of ideals. The fact is constantly mentioned in the more expensive monthly magazines, and has reached the provincial pulpits, I am told. And my ideal has always been to love someone of the name of Ernest. There is something in that name that inspires absolute confidence." She is very firm about this, and Cecily, whose words on the subject are almost identical, is nearly as firm. The comic parallel generates a certain irony against the girls; we are tempted to laugh at them for sharing a folly, yet we cannot help admiring the strength of their resolution, absurd though it is. Though idealism is burlesqued, we are made to admire the wit and courage required to impose a pattern on the world, even such a one as this.

The women in the play are generally stronger and more resourceful than the men. The latter are forced to prevaricate in a way that at times seems shuffling, even abject, whereas the former are always perfectly poised and move with imperturbable grace from one contradictory posture to another. I suspect that this has something to do with Wilde's own personality and personal history, but the pattern makes sense on its own terms. The play may be seen as a disquisition in favor of a set of attitudes more normally associated with women than with men. It commends the sort of character that accepts experience, with all its confusions, and accommodates itself through provisional opportunist adjustments—through style, in short. It pokes fun at hard and fast ideas about reality, at that aggressive kind of intelligence which seeks to control reality through theory. Rightly or wrongly, women are thought of as conforming more often to the subtle stereotype; men are thought of as conforming more often to the aggressive stereotype. Wilde was not simplistic about this. The embodiment of aggressive masculine intelligence in the play is Miss Prism, but that is part of the joke against her. The other women are naturally more at home in Wilde's world than the men.

CHAPTER 4

Genre and Structure in *The Importance of Being Earnest*

READINGS ON
THE IMPORTANCE
OF BEING EARNEST

Wilde's Use of Ironic Counterpoint

Eric Bentley

Eric Bentley writes that *The Importance of Being Earnest* is about false seriousness, priggishness, and hypocrisy. According to Bentley, Wilde presents a new type of comedy, one that is not dependent on plot and character. Instead, Wilde offers an unbroken stream of dialogue that dances around but never directly attacks the problems of society. Wilde skims over topics like death, money, beauty, morals, the class system, and truth, taking verbal shots as he goes. Bentley maintains that Wilde hovers on the edge of criticism throughout the play, but never really crosses over.

Bentley argues that Wilde's witticisms are not comic: rather, they serve as ironic counterpoints to the absurdities of the action. This counterpoint is also seen in the characters, who display a great contrast between their surface elegance and the silliness of what they do. Bentley writes that there is always a great contrast between the assured appearances of the characters and their inner emptiness.

Eric Bentley is a professor of theater at State University of New York at Buffalo. He is the author of *What Is Theatre?* and *The Life of the Drama.*

The Importance of Being Earnest (1895) is a variant, not of domestic drama like *Candida* or of melodrama like *Brassbound* [plays by George Bernard Shaw], but of farce, a genre which, being the antithesis of serious, is not easily put to serious uses. In fact nothing is easier than to handle this play without noticing what it contains. It is so consistently farcical in tone, characterization, and plot that very few care to root out any more serious content. The general conclusion has been that Wilde merely decorates a silly play with a flippant wit. Like [Irish dramatist George Bernard] Shaw he is dismissed as "not really a dramatist at all." Unlike Shaw he does not have any such dramatic structure to offer in refutation of his critics as underlies a *Major Barbara* or a *Candida.* We cannot turn to him for the dialectical steel frame of a [French comic dramatist] Molière or a Shaw. Yet we shall only display our own insensitivity if we dismiss him.

Insensitivity to slight and delicate things is insensitivity *tout court.* That is what Wilde meant when he declared that the man who despises superficiality is himself superficial. His best play is connected with this idea. As its title confesses, it is about *earnestness,* that is, Victorian solemnity, that kind of false seriousness which means priggishness, hypocrisy, and lack of irony. Wilde proclaims that earnestness is less praiseworthy than the ironic attitude to life which is regarded as superficial. His own art and the comic spirit which [English dramatist William] Congreve embodied and which [English novelist George] Meredith had described, were thereby vindicated. Wilde calls *The Importance of Being Earnest* "a trivial comedy for serious people" meaning, in the first place, a comedy which will be thought negligible by the earnest and, in the second, a *comedy of surface* for connoisseurs. The latter will perceive that Wilde is as much of a moralist as Bernard Shaw but that, instead of presenting the problems of modern society directly, he flits around them, teasing them, declining to grapple with them. His wit is no searchlight into the darkness of modern life. It is a flickering, a coruscation, intermittently revealing the upper class of England in a harsh bizarre light. This upper class could feel about Shaw that at least he took them seriously, no one more so. But the outrageous Oscar (whom they took care to get rid of as they had got rid of Byron) refused to see the importance of being earnest.

WILDE'S TOPIC SKIMMING

One does not find Wilde's satire embedded in plot and character as in traditional high comedy. It is a running accompaniment to the play, and this fact, far from indicating immaturity, is the making of a new sort of comedy. The plot is one of those Gilbertian [English dramatist Sir William] absurdities of lost infants and recovered brothers which can only be thought of to be laughed at. Yet the dialogue which sustains the plot, or is sustained by it, is an unbroken stream of comment on all the themes of life which the plot is so far from broaching. Perhaps *comment* is too flat and downright a conception. Wildean "comment" is a pseudo-irresponsible jabbing at all the great problems, and we would be justified in removing the prefix "pseudo" if the Wildean satire, for all its naughtiness, had not a cumulative effect and a paradoxical one. Flippancies repeated, developed, and, so to say, elaborated almost into a system amount to something in the end—and thereby cease to be flippant. What begins as a prank ends as a criticism of life. What begins as intellectual high-kicking ends as intellectual sharp-shooting.

The margins of an annotated copy of *The Importance* would show such headings as: death; money and marriage; the nature of style; ideology and economics; beauty and truth; the psychology of philanthropy; the decline of aristocracy; nineteenth-century morals; the class system. The possibility of such notations in itself means little. But if we bear in mind that Wilde is skimming steadily over mere topics all through *The Importance,* we can usefully turn to a particular page to see precisely how this works. To choose the opening page is not to load the dice in a dramatist's favor, since that page is usually either heavy-going exposition or mere patter which allows the audience to get seated. Here is Wilde's first page:

ALGERNON: Did you hear what I was playing, Lane?

LANE: I didn't think it polite to listen, sir.

ALGERNON: I'm sorry for that, for your sake. I don't play accurately—anyone can play accurately—but I play with wonderful expression. As far as the piano is concerned sentiment is my forte. I keep science for life.

LANE: Yes, sir.

ALGERNON: And, speaking of the science of Life, have you got the cucumber sandwiches cut for Lady Bracknell?

LANE: Yes, sir.

ALGERNON: Oh! . . . by the way, Lane, I see from your book that on Thursday night, when Lord Sherman and Mr. Worthing were dining with me, eight bottles of champagne are entered as having been consumed.

LANE: Yes, sir; eight bottles and a pint.

ALGERNON: Why is it that at a bachelor's establishment the servants invariably drink the champagne? I ask merely for information.

LANE: I attribute it to the superior quality of the wine, sir. I have often observed that in married households the champagne is rarely of a first-rate brand.

ALGERNON: Good heavens! Is marriage so demoralizing as that?

LANE: I believe it *is* a very pleasant state, sir. I have had very little experience of it myself up to the present. I have only been married once. That was in consequence of a misunderstanding between myself and a young person.

ALGERNON: I don't know that I am much interested in your family life, Lane.

LANE: No, sir. It is not a very interesting subject. I never think of it myself.

ALGERNON: Very natural, I am sure. That will do, Lane, thank you.

LANE: Thank you, sir. (*He goes out*)

ALGERNON: Lane's views on marriage seem somewhat lax. Really, if the lower orders don't set us a good example, what on earth is the use of them? They seem, as a class, to have absolutely no sense of moral responsibility.

This passage is enough to show the way in which Wilde attaches a serious and satirical allusion to every remark. The butler's "I didn't think it polite to listen, sir" is a prelude to the jokes against class society which run through the play. Algernon's first little speech touches on the foolish opposition of life and sentiment, science and art. Talk of science and life leads by Wildean transition back to the action and the cucumber sandwiches. Champagne takes the action to speculation on servants and masters, and thence to marriage and morals. A little dialectical climax is reached with the answer to the question: "Is marriage so demoralizing as that?" when Lane coolly replies: "I believe it *is* a very pleasant state, sir," and adds, by way of an explanation no less disconcerting by Victorian standards, "I have had very little experience of it myself up to the present. I have only been married once." Which is followed by the explanation of the explanation: "That was in consequence of a misunderstanding. . . ." It cannot be said that marriage in this passage receives the "staggering blows" which the ardent reformer is wont to administer. But does it not receive poisoned pin pricks that are just as effective? Are not the inversions and double inversions of standards managed with dexterous delicacy? "No, sir. It is not a very interesting subject." A delicious turn in the argument! And then the little moralistic summing-up of Algernon's: "Lane's views on marriage seem somewhat lax. Really, if the lower orders don't set us a good example. . . ." And so it ripples on.

We are accustomed to plays in which a serious plot and

theme are enlivened—"dramatized," as we say—by comic incident and witticism. Such plays are at best sweetened pills. "Entertainment value" is added as an afterthought, reminding one of the man who, having watched for weeks the construction of a modern Gothic building, cried one day: "Oh, look, they're putting the architecture on now!" Oscar Wilde's procedure is the opposite of all this. He has no serious plot, no credible characters. His witticisms are not comic, but serious relief. They are in ironic counterpoint with the absurdities of the action. This counterpoint is Wilde's method. It is what gives him his peculiar voice and his peculiar triumph. It is what makes him hard to catch: the fish's tail flicks, flashes, and disappears. Perhaps *The Importance* should be defined as "almost a satire." As the conversations in *Alice in Wonderland* hover on the frontier of sense without ever quite crossing it, so the dialogue in *The Importance* is forever on the frontier of satire, forever on the point of breaking into bitter criticism. It never breaks. The ridiculous action constantly steps in to prevent the break. That is its function. Before the enemy can denounce Wilde the agile outburst is over and we are back among the cucumber sandwiches.

The counterpoint or irony of Wilde's play expresses itself theatrically in the contrast between the elegance and *savoir-faire* of the actors and the absurdity of what they actually do. This contrast too can be dismissed as mere Oscarism and frivolity. Actually it is integral to an uncommonly rich play. The contrast between smooth, assured appearances and inner emptiness is, moreover, nothing more nor less than a fact of sociology and history. Wilde knew his England. He knew her so well that he could scarcely be surprised when she laughed off his truisms as paradoxes and fastened a humorless and baleful eye on all his flights of fancy. Wilde had his own solution to the problem stated by Meredith, the problem of finding a vantage point for satire in an unaristocratic age. It was the solution of Bohemianism. For Wilde the Bohemian attitude was far from being a philosophy in itself —a point which most of his friends and enemies, beginning at the Wilde trial, seem to have missed. Bohemianism was for Wilde a mask. To wear masks was Wilde's personal adjustment to modern life, as it was [German philosopher Friedrich] Nietzsche's. Hence we are right in talking of his pose as we are right in talking of Nietzsche's vanity. The mistake is in believing that these men deceived themselves. If we patronize them the joke is on us. If Wilde seems shallow when we want depth, if he seems a liar when we want truth, we should recall his words: "A Truth in Art is that whose contradictory is also true. The Truths of metaphysics are the Truths of masks." These words lead us to Pirandello.

The Tedium of *The Importance of Being Earnest*

Mary McCarthy

Mary McCarthy writes that Wilde not only imposes himself and his opinions on his audience, but also outstays his welcome. She suggests that Wilde's outrageousness becomes monotonous. The play's tedium is exemplified in act 2, where the joke of gluttony surrounding the muffins has, according to McCarthy, already been exhausted in the first act with the cucumber sandwiches. She criticizes the playwright for including in the play private jokes for the bisexual man that are lost on the audience.

McCarthy argues that Wilde's stock characters become stock jokes and the formula for the humor is like a detective story device in which paradox is used to shock the audience. Insensitivity is the comic "vice" of the characters and selfishness is their moral alternative. McCarthy claims that the play has the tone of emotionally bankrupt people imprisoned in a world of comfort. All of the characters have different shades of depravity, but none can compare to the insensitivity of Lady Bracknell, who epitomizes effrontery.

Novelist, influential literary critic, and essayist, Mary McCarthy taught English at Sarah Lawrence College, Bronxville, New York, and lectured at University College, University of London.

One of Oscar Wilde's acquaintances wrote of him that he could never be quite a gentleman because he dressed too well and his manners were too polished. The same criticism can be made of his art. There is something *outré* in all of Wilde's work that makes one sympathize to a degree with the Marquess of Queensberry [the father of Wilde's young friend, Lord Alfred Douglas]; this fellow is really insufferable. Oscar's real sin (and the one for which society punished him, homosexuality being merely the blotter charge) was making himself too much at home. This is as readily seen in his comedies as in his epigrammatic indorsement of socialism or his call on a Colorado coal mine. He was overly familiar with his subjects. [Irish dramatist George Bernard] Shaw said of him that he did not know enough about art to justify his parade of aestheticism. Certainly, he was not intimate enough with poverty to style himself an enemy of riches. In this light, the Marquess of Queensberry's libel, that he went about "posing" as a sodomist, speaks, in the plain man's language, the true word of damnation. In his comedies, it is his audience whose acquaintance he presumes on. Where the usual work of art invites the spectator into its world, already furnished and habitable, Wilde's plays do just the opposite: the author invites himself and his fast opinions into the world of the spectator. He ensconces himself with intolerable freedom and always outstays his sufferance—the trouble with Wilde's wit is that it does not recognize when the party is over. The effect of this effrontery is provoking in both senses; the outrageous has its own monotony, and insolence can only strike once.

THE PLAY'S TEDIUM

In *The Importance of Being Earnest* (Royale Theatre), the tedium is concentrated in the second act, where two young ladies are rude to each other over tea and cake, and two young gentlemen follow them being selfish about the muffins. The joke of gluttony and the joke of rudeness (which are really the same one, for heartlessness is the basic pleasantry) have been exhausted in the first act: nothing can be said by the muffin that has not already been said by the cucumber sandwich. The thin little joke that remains, the importance of the name Ernest for matrimony, is in its visible aspects insufficiently entertaining. That the joke about the name Ernest is doubtless a private one makes it less endurable to the audience, which is pointedly left out of the fun. To the bisexual man, it was perhaps deliciously comic that a man should have one name, the tamest in English, for his wife and female relations, and another for his male friends, for trips and "lost" weekends; but Wilde was a prude—he went to law to clear his character—and the anti-social jibe dwindles on the stage to a refined and incomprehensible titter.

Yet, in spite of the exhausting triviality of the second act, *The Importance of Being Earnest* is Wilde's most original play. It has the character of a ferocious idyl. Here, for the first time, the subject of Wilde's comedy coincides with its climate; there is no more pretense of emotion. The unwed mother, his stock "serious" heroine, here becomes a stock joke—"Shall there be a different standard for women than for men?" cries Mr. Jack Worthing, flinging himself on the governess, Miss Prism, who had checked him accidentally in a valise at a railroad station twenty-five years before. In *The Importance of Being Earnest* the title is a *blague,* and virtue disappears from the Wilde stage, as though jerked off by one of those hooks that were used in the old days of vaudeville to remove an unsuccessful performer. Depravity is the hero and the only character, the people on the stage embodying various shades of it. It is deepest dyed in the pastoral region of respectability and innocence. The London *roué* is artless simplicity itself beside the dreadnought society dowager, and she, in her turn, is out-brazened by her debutante daughter, and she by the country miss, and she by her spectacled governess, till finally the village rector with his clerical clothes, his vow of celibacy, and his sermon on the manna, adjustable to all occasions, slithers noiselessly into the rose garden, specious as the Serpent Himself.

WILDE'S COMIC FORMULA

The formula of this humor is the same as that of the detective story: the culprit is the man with the most guileless appearance. Normal expectations are methodically inverted, and the structure of the play is the simple structure of the paradox. Like the detective story, like the paradox, this play is a shocker. It is pure sport of the mind, and hence very nearly "English." The clergyman is the fox; the governess the vixen; and the young bloods are out for the kill. Humanitarian considerations are out of place here; they belong to the middle class. Insensibility is the comic "vice" of the characters; it is also their charm and badge of prestige. Selfishness and servility are the moral alternatives presented; the sinister impression made by the governess and the rector comes partly from their rectitude and partly from their menial demeanor. Algernon Moncrieff and Cecily Cardew are, taken by themselves, unendurable; the meeching Dr. Chasuble, however, justifies their way of life by affording a comparison—it is better to be cruel than craven.

Written on the brink of his fall, *The Importance of Being Earnest* is Wilde's true *De Profundis*; the other was false sentiment. This is hell, and if a great deal of it is tiresome, eternity is, as M. Sartre says, a bore. The tone of the Wilde dialogue, inappropriate to the problem drama, perfectly reflects conditions in this infernal Arcadia; peevish, fretful, valetudinarian, it is the tone of an elderly recluse who lives imprisoned by his comforts; it combines the finicky and the greedy, like a piggish old lady.

LADY BRACKNELL'S INSENSITIVITY

Fortunately, however, for everyone, there is a goddess in the play. The great lumbering dowager, Lady Augusta Bracknell, traveling to the country in a luggage-train, is the only character thick and rudimentary enough to be genuinely wellborn. Possibly because of her birth, she has a certain Olympian freedom. When she is on the stage—during the first and the third acts—the play opens up. The epigram, which might be defined as the *desire* to say something witty, falters before her majesty. Her own rumbling speech is unpredictable; anything may come out of her. Where the other characters are hard as nails, Lady Augusta is rock. She is so insensitive that the spoken word reaches her slowly, from an immeasurable distance, as if she were deaf. Into this splendid creation, Wilde surely put all the feelings of admiration and despair aroused in him by Respectability. This citadel of the arbitrary was for him the Castle; he remarked, in his later years, that he would have been glad to marry Queen Victoria. Lady Augusta is the one character he could ever really imagine, partly, no doubt, because she could not imagine *him*. Her effrontery surpasses his by being perfectly unconscious; she cannot impose on the audience for she does not know they are there. She is named, oddly enough, after Bracknell, the country address of the Marchioness of Queensberry, where Wilde, as it turned out, was less at home than he fancied. The irony of the pastoral setting was apparently not lost on the Marquess of Queensberry, who arrived at the first night with a bunch of turnips and carrots.

The Importance of Being Earnest as Self-Parody

Christopher S. Nassaar

Christopher S. Nassaar argues that *The Importance of Being Earnest* is Wilde's private joke made public. The playwright mines his career and previous works for intellectual content he reduces to harmlessness and even absurdity. For example, in his novel *Dorian Gray* the main character fears the horror of the exposure of his wicked double life. According to Nassaar, this double life is parodied in *The Importance of Being Earnest* when the unmasking of Jack and Algy does not lead to shame but to marriage. In the play *Salome* the protagonist feasts on the head of the slain Iokanaan. Nassaar maintains that Salome's sexual appetite is parodied by Algy's mild gluttony. Finally, in *An Ideal Husband* Mrs. Chevely is exposed as a thief when her lost bracelet is found. In *The Importance of Being Earnest* this is parodied when Jack loses his cigarette case and is trapped and exposed. However, instead of suffering defeat like Mrs. Cheveley, Jack simply finds a friend in Algy and all proves to be harmless.

Christopher S. Nassaar is a professor of English at American University of Beirut, Lebanon. He is an editor and the author of *York Notes on English Literature: Oscar Wilde.*

In *The Importance of Being Earnest,* Wilde's reaction against the demon universe takes a different form, and one more uniquely his own. The two most prominent words in the play are *nonsense* and *serious,* or their synonyms. This is entirely appropriate, since the play itself is a reduction of all se-

Excerpted from *Into the Demon Universe: A Literary Exploration of Oscar Wilde,* by Christopher S. Nassaar. Copyright © 1974 by Yale University. Reprinted with permission from Yale University Press.

riousness to the level of nonsense. In it, Wilde pauses for a space, takes a hard look at his career to date, and has a good, long laugh at himself. The play is absolutely devoid of sober content, and any attempt to find serious meaning in it must of necessity fall wide of the mark.

To say that the play has no serious meaning, however, is not to say that it has no meaning at all. Its very message, paradoxically, lies in its lack of seriousness, for here Oscar Wilde has a hearty laugh at his own expense. The target of the fun is Wilde's work up to this time. "Lord Arthur Savile's Crime," *The Picture of Dorian Gray, Salome, A Woman of No Importance,* even *An Ideal Husband*—Wilde singles out these works and, one by one, destroys their intellectual content, reducing them to the level of harmlessness and absurdity. Quite earnestly, he informs us that every serious thought he has had to date is nonsense—and very laughable nonsense at that.

THE PLAY AS A PRIVATE JOKE

The Importance of Being Earnest is essentially a private joke, though the source of its great popularity is Wilde's ability to translate the joke into public terms. By achieving and maintaining a perfect balance between the public and the private, Wilde managed to write one of the most brilliant comic masterpieces of the nineteenth century.

Oscar Wilde's works are often based on earlier ones. *The Picture of Dorian Gray* carefully counterpoints "Lord Arthur Savile's Crime" while providing *Lady Windermere's Fan* with its basic theme. *A Woman of No Importance* is thematically a repetition of *Salome,* while its wit is borrowed largely from *Dorian Gray. An Ideal Husband* harks back to the fairy tales in theme. *The Importance of Being Earnest* is the least self-contained of Wilde's works, for it is rooted not in one but in practically all of them. It is, moreover, an entirely original play. Wilde was later to write, in *De Profundis:* "I took the drama, the most objective form known to art, and I made it as personal a mode of expression as the lyric or the sonnet, at the same time that I widened its range and enriched its characterization."

If *Earnest* has exasperated the critics, it is because of this complete originality. Without doubt, it widened the range of the drama. Drama had been used subjectively before, by the Romantics, but Wilde here carried it to the outer limits of subjectivity and thus provided us with probably the most personal, private play in existence—a play that is basically a self-parody. Forever a lover of paradox, he took the most objective form known to literature and treated it entirely subjectively. The opening lines suggest what sort of a drama this is going to be:

> ALGERNON: Did you hear what I was playing, Lane?
>
> LANE: I didn't think it polite to listen, sir.
>
> ALGERNON: I'm sorry for that, for your sake. I don't play accurately—any one can play accurately—but I play with wonderful expression. As far as the piano is concerned, sentiment is my forte.

Algy's piano-playing is an art, but he aims through it purely to express a mood. Lane regards this art as private and discreetly turns a deaf ear, but had he listened he would have had an enjoyable experience.

Like Algy's piano-playing, *The Importance of Being Earnest* aims purely at creating a mood, and it succeeds so brilliantly that audiences have been applauding since 1895. It is the object of this analysis to show that the play also has a private meaning that is wholly consistent with its humorous trivial mood. The meaning—not necessary to an enjoyment of *Earnest*—reinforces the mood and adds an extra comic dimension to the play. To see the play's dialogue as constituting an anti-Victorian barrage—as [critic] Eric Bentley does—or to condemn it as depraved—as [critic] Mary McCarthy does—is really to be untrue to its tone and unappreciative of its originality. Even Richard Ellmann misses the mark—though not by much—when he sees the play's theme as being sin and crime, treated indifferently and rendered harmless.

WILDE'S PARODY OF "LORD ARTHUR SAVILE'S CRIME"

Wilde parodies his earlier works haphazardly in *Earnest*, but in examining the play it is more organized to discuss these works in order of their composition. In "Lord Arthur Savile's Crime," Sybil was the erotic personification of all perfection, and Arthur had to undergo a symbolic baptism and murder the evil within himself in order to marry her. Gwendolyn and Cecily exist in this play partly—even entirely—as parodies of Sybil. Both dismiss any attempt on the part of their suitors to consider them perfect. For example:

JACK: You're quite perfect, Miss Fairfax.

GWENDOLYN: Oh! I hope I am not that. It would leave no room for developments, and I intend to develop in many directions.

Algy has a similar experience with Cecily:

ALGERNON: I hope, Cecily, I shall not offend you if I state quite frankly and openly that you seem to me to be in every way the visible personification of absolute perfection.

CECILY: I think your frankness does you great credit, Ernest. If you will allow me, I will copy your remarks into my diary.

Cecily comically undercuts the notion of her perfection by vainly dashing off to copy Algy's remarks into her diary. Her vanity is elaborated at some length in the original, four-act version of the play, which Wilde trimmed down for the stage at the insistence of George Alexander.

Indeed, any idea we may have had about the perfection of Cecily and Gwendolyn is dispelled by their verbal duel in act 2. Furthermore, they both end up with wicked husbands. Sybil—or Lady Chiltern, for that matter—would have died as a result, but Cecily and Gwendolyn remain quite happy and unharmed at the end of the play. Vice is a delightful, harmless thing in *Earnest:* it cannot destroy. Besides, a touch of wickedness in a man makes him all the more attractive, and Cecily's interest in Algy had begun when she heard how bad he was. . . .

In *Earnest, The Soul of Man Under Socialism* is cut to pieces in a few brief lines. In the essay, Wilde had advocated the abolition of private property and had tried to win over the rich by writing: "Property not only has duties, but has so many duties that its possession to any large extent is a bore. It involves endless claims upon one, endless attention to business, endless bother. If property had simply pleasures we could stand it; but its duties make it unbearable. In the interest of the rich we must get rid of it." In *The Importance of Being Earnest,* the wealthy Lady Bracknell agrees with Wilde but finds a nonsocialistic solution to the problem:

LADY BRACKNELL: What is your income?

JACK: Between seven and eight thousand a year.

LADY BRACKNELL: (*Makes a note in her book.*) In land, or in investments?

JACK: In investments, chiefly.

LADY BRACKNELL: That is satisfactory. What between the duties expected of one during one's lifetime, and the duties exacted from one after one's death, land has ceased to be either a profit or a pleasure. It gives one position, and prevents one from keeping it up. That's all that can be said about land.

If private property is a bother, then by all means eliminate it—invest the money! As for the lower classes, whose poverty Wilde had seen in the essay as poisoning the lives of the rich, they are summarily dismissed at the beginning of the play when Algy says: "Lane's views on marriage seem somewhat lax. Really, if the lower classes don't set us a good example, what on earth is the use of them? They seem, as a class, to have absolutely no sense of moral responsibility." Nor does Lady Bracknell seem at all upset about the existence of the lower classes. After all, they are not on her list of socially acceptable people—the same list as the duchess of Bolton's, no less! If Jack cannot produce socially acceptable parents, he cannot marry Gwendolyn, and that is the end of that. . . .

WILDE'S PARODY OF *THE PICTURE OF DORIAN GRAY*

The Picture of Dorian Gray is also heavily parodied in *The Importance of Being Earnest*. Dorian led a double life. The picture of his soul was locked safely away in a dark room while the innocent face he presented to respectable society was only a mask. As society began to suspect the real Dorian, he found himself shunned and avoided. His total unmasking—a horror he is spared during his lifetime—would have meant his irrevocable social ruin. Jack and Algy also lead double lives. As with Dorian, their real self is the wicked one. Jack explains to Algy that he wears a mask in the country for the sake of his ward, Cecily: "When one is placed in the position of guardian, one has to adopt a very high moral tone on all subjects. It's one's duty to do so."

Algy, on the other hand, assumes his façade in the city, where he is constantly under the gaze of Lady Bracknell and other respectable personages. The mask drops only when he goes Bunburying. As the play moves to its climax, the respectable identities of Jack and Algy are discovered by all to be fictional. Jack is found out—he is Ernest. Algy is also found out—he is Jack's wicked younger brother Ernest. For both Ernests, however, the result of this revelation is not ostracism but marriage. By reducing Dorian's situation to the level of farce and turning the unmasking into a happy event, Wilde dismisses the protagonist of his novel with a roar of carefree laughter. . . .

WILDE'S PARODY OF *SALOME*

A good deal of the fun in *The Importance of Being Earnest* is directed against *Salome*. A huge Negro executioner brought Iokanaan's head to Salome on a silver shield, and she lustfully proceeded to feast upon it. This gruesome event is parodied when Lane brings Algernon some cucumber sandwiches on a salver, and he gluttonously devours them all and remains hungry. Algy's action is not quite proper, as the sandwiches were intended for Lady Bracknell. Far from being crushed between huge salvers, moreover, Algy lives to dine again, first at Willis's, then on muffins at Jack's country home.

In the four-act version of the play, Jack too has a huge appetite. Masquerading as Ernest in the city, he has run up a tremendous food bill at the Savoy—£762 14s. 2d., to be precise—and finally a bailiff appears at Jack's country home to arrest Mr. Ernest Worthing. Algy, who is Bunburying in the country as Ernest, finds himself in deep trouble and is almost carted off to Holloway prison, but Cecily intervenes, and finally Jack is persuaded to step in and rescue Algy by paying the bill he himself had really run up at the Savoy. So Salome's insatiable, hellish sexual appetite is reduced in *Earnest* to the level of mild gluttony. Whereas Salome meets death for yielding to her uncontrollable appetite, Jack and Algy both escape punishment in *Earnest*. Wilde dismisses Salome with a peal of laughter, declaring that her hunger was, after all, nonsense. She would have done better to order some cucumber sandwiches—or to have gone, perhaps, to Willis's or even the Savoy! . . .

WILDE'S PARODY OF *AN IDEAL HUSBAND*

Finally, in *An Ideal Husband*, Mrs. Cheveley lost a snake-bracelet and Lord Goring found it. When she tried to reclaim the bracelet, she was trapped, exposed as a thief, threatened with the police, and defeated. Similarly, Jack loses a cigarette-case and Algernon finds it. When Jack moves to reclaim his case, Algy discovers that Jack is "one of the most advanced Bunburyists" he knows. In one of the funniest episodes in *The Importance of Being Earnest*, Jack is trapped and exposed; but the result is that he gets his cigarette-case back and deepens his friendship with a fellow-Bunburyist. What had proved lethal for Mrs. Cheveley proves advantageous for

Jack. Indeed, everything can be counted on to prove harmless in this never-never land of farce, Wilde's funniest and most delightful play.

Oscar Wilde was the type of subjective writer who always put himself into his works. He was later to write to Lord Douglas: "You knew what my Art was to me, the great primal note by which I had revealed, first myself to myself, and then myself to the world." Even this fact is parodied in *The Importance of Being Earnest*, when Cecily says of her diary: "It is simply a very young girl's record of her own thoughts and impressions, and consequently meant for publication."

CHRONOLOGY

1854

Oscar Wilde is born in Dublin on October 16.

1864–71

Wilde attends Portora Royal School, Enniskillen.

1871–74

Wilde attends Trinity College, Dublin, where he wins numerous academic prizes.

1876

Sir William Wilde, Oscar's father, dies.

1877

Wilde travels through Europe with Professor Mahaffy.

1878

Wilde wins the Newdigate Prize for his poem "Ravenna."

1880

Wilde prints his first play *Vera; or the Nihilists.*

1881-82

Wilde lectures across America.

1884

Wilde marries Constance Lloyd in London.

1885

Wilde's first son, Cyril, is born.

1886

Wilde's second son, Vyvyan, is born.

1888

Wilde's fairy stories, *The Happy Prince and Other Tales,* are published.

1890

The Picture of Dorian Gray is first published in *Lippincott's Magazine*.

1891

Wilde meets Lord Alfred Douglas; publishes "The Soul of Man Under Socialism" and in Paris Wilde writes *Salome*.

1892

Lady Windermere's Fan is staged but London censors ban *Salome*.

1893

A Woman of No Importance is produced.

1895

Both *An Ideal Husband* and *The Importance of Being Earnest* are produced; Wilde sues Alfred Douglas's father, the Marquess of Queensberry, for libel; Wilde loses his case and is subsequently arrested for sexual offenses.

1895-97

Wilde is imprisoned at Reading Gaol for sexual offenses.

1896

Wilde's mother dies.

1897

Wilde writes *De Profundis* and travels throughout Europe.

1898

Constance Wilde dies; Wilde publishes *The Ballad of Reading Gaol*.

1900

Wilde dies in a rundown hotel in Paris on November 30.

For Further Research

Works by Oscar Wilde

The Ballad of Reading Gaol. London: Leonard Smithers, 1898.
De Profundis. London: Methuen, 1905.
The Duchess of Padua: A Tragedy of the XVI Century. Paris: Privately Printed, 1883.
The Happy Prince and Other Tales. London: David Nutt, 1888.
An Ideal Husband. London: Leonard Smithers, 1899.
The Importance of Being Earnest: A Trivial Comedy for Serious People. London: Leonard Smithers, 1899.
Lady Windermere's Fan: A Play About a Good Woman. London: Elkin Mathews and John Lane, 1893.
The Picture of Dorian Gray. London and New York: Ward Lock, 1891.
Ravenna. Oxford, England: Thos. Shrimpton and Son, 1878.
Salome. A Tragedy in One Act. London: Elkin Mathews and John Lane, 1893.
The Soul of Man Under Socialism. London: Printed Privately, 1895.
A Woman of No Importance in *Two Society Comedies.* London: John Lane, 1894.

Collections of Wilde's Work

The Artist as Critic: Critical Writings of Oscar Wilde. Ed. Richard Ellmann. New York: Random House, 1969.
The Complete Shorter Fiction of Oscar Wilde. Ed. Isobel Murray. Oxford, England: Oxford University Press, 1979.
The Letters of Oscar Wilde. Ed. Rupert Hart-Davis. New York: Harcourt, Brace & World, 1962.
More Letters of Oscar Wilde. Ed. Rupert Hart-Davis. New York: Vanguard, 1985.
Oscar Wilde's Oxford Notebooks. Ed. Philip E. Smith and Michael S. Helfand. New York: Oxford University Press, 1989.
The Writings of Oscar Wilde. Ed. Isobel Murray. Oxford, England: Oxford University Press, 1989.

BIOGRAPHICAL WORKS ABOUT OSCAR WILDE

Lord Alfred Douglas, *Oscar Wilde and Myself.* London: John Long, 1914.

Richard Ellmann, *Oscar Wilde.* New York: Vintage Books, 1987.

Martin Fido, *Oscar Wilde.* London: Hamlyn, 1973.

Frank Harris, *Oscar Wilde: His Life and Confessions.* New York: Covici, Friede, 1930.

Phillipe Jullian, *Oscar Wilde.* New York: Viking, 1968.

Melissa Knox, *Oscar Wilde: A Long and Lovely Suicide.* New Haven, CT: Yale University Press, 1994.

Louis Kronenberger, *Oscar Wilde.* Boston: Little, Brown, 1976.

Robert Miller, *Oscar Wilde.* New York: Frederick Ungar, 1982.

Edouard Roditi, *Oscar Wilde.* Norfolk, CT: New Directions, 1947.

Robert H. Sherard, *The Life of Oscar Wilde.* London: Laurie, 1906.

ABOUT *THE IMPORTANCE OF BEING EARNEST* AND WILDE'S PLAYS

Harold Bloom, ed., *Modern Critical Views: Oscar Wilde.* New York: Chelsea House, 1985.

Davis Coakely, *Oscar Wilde: The Importance of Being Irish.* Dublin: Town House, 1994.

Philip K. Cohen, *The Moral Vision of Oscar Wilde.* London: Associated University Presses, 1976.

San Juan Epifanio Jr., *The Art of Oscar Wilde.* Princeton, NJ: Princeton University Press, 1967.

Donald H. Ericksen, *Oscar Wilde.* New York: Twayne, 1977.

William Green, "Wilde and the Bunburys," *Modern Drama,* 1978.

Christopher S. Nassaar, *Into the Demon Universe: A Literary Exploration of Oscar Wilde.* New Haven, CT: Yale University Press, 1974.

Kerry Powell, *Oscar Wilde and the Theatre of the 1890s.* New York: Cambridge University Press, 1990.

Arthur Ransome, *Oscar Wilde: A Critical Study.* London: Methuen, 1913.

Alvin Redman, ed., *The Wit and Humor of Oscar Wilde.* Princeton, NJ: Princeton University Press, 1967.

Katharine Worth, *Oscar Wilde.* New York: Grove, 1984.

INDEX

Adorno, Theodor, 56
"Advisability of Not Being
Brought Up in a Hand-Bag,
The" (Leverson), 72
Alexander, George, 48, 65
attention to detail, 66–67
playing Jack Worthing, 26
and prosecution of Marquis
of Queensberry, 87
requesting revisions, 106
Wilde's displeasure on
editorial changes by, 102
Wilde's letter and play to,
107
Anderson, Mary, 20
Archer, William, 77, 115
Arnold, Matthew, 20, 133
attire
and dandyism, 142
of Oscar Wilde, 19
in Victorian England, 134–35
for women, 22
Auden, W.H., 45
audience
"in" on epigrammatic
jokes, 61
manipulation of, 86–87, 89
Wilde imposing his
opinions on, 167–68

Ballad of Reading Gaol, The,
31

Baudelaire, Charles, 142–43,
148
Beckett, Samuel, 56
Beerbohm, Max, 75
Behrendt, Patricia Flanagan,
83
Benjamin, Walter, 53
Bentley, Eric, 35, 45–46, 50,
88, 161, 173
Berkeley Gold Medal for
Greek, 18
Bernhardt, Sarah, 15, 24
Bird, Alan, 42, 101
Bristow, Joseph, 91
Brown, Julia Prewitt, 51
Bunbury, Henry Shirley,
78–79, 80, 82
Bunbury, Sir Edward
Herbert, 79–82

Carson, Edward, 29
Celimaire (Labiche), 45
Cenci, The (Shelley), 133
Chaplin, Charlie, 54
characters
Algernon Moncrieff, 36
appetite in, 176
christening of, 49
dandyism in, 144
decadence in, 73
deception by, 46
desire to escape, 93–94

eating cucumber
  sandwiches, 95
on the female sex, 111
fictional alias of, 39, 93
on flirting with one's
  husband, 86
impulse in, 155
as Jack's real brother, 42
on Jack's two selves,
  38–39
Lady Bracknell on, 100
on lower classes, 175
on marriage, 163–64
mocking Gwendolen's
  learning, 106
as moving back in time,
  55–56
posing as Ernest, 40, 47
preconceptions by, 129
proposal to Cecily, 40–41
real identity revealed, 175
on relations/family, 153
relationship with Jack ,
  91–92
on romance/marriage,
  112–13
Bunbury, 93
based on
  Henry Shirley Bunbury,
    78–79
  Sir Edward Herbert
    Bunbury, 79–82
as dying, 130
homosexual connotations
  in name of, 76–77
as name of English
  village, 77–78
reaction to death of, 117
source of name for, 75–76,
  82
symbolism in, 137
Cecily Cardew, 37, 39, 40
Algy's proposal to, 40–41
artificiality of, 120–22

changes in, after
  revisions, 107–10
dandyism in, 145, 147–48,
  150
deceit by, 47
discovering truth about
  Ernest, 41
on equal terms with men,
  110–11
impulse in, 155
on marriage, 111–12
motive for marriage, 112
on name Ernest, 99, 115
perfection in, 173–74
preconceptions by, 129–30
rejecting notion of
  antithesis, 136
childlikeness of, 51–52
criticism of, 35
denying substantiality of
  love, 156
Dr. Chasuble, 40, 41
on christening, 49
dandyism in, 140–41, 145
source of name for, 75
Ernest (fictional)
finding truth about, 41
liking name of, 39
and pun on "Earnest,"
  87–89, 94–95, 115, 152,
  153
tediousness in joke of, 168
fantasies of, 158–59
gender differences in, 159
Gwendolen Fairfax, 36–37
artificiality of, 120–22
attitude toward the family,
  154
changeability in, 155
changes in, from
  revisions, 106–107
dandyism in, 148, 149–50
determinism in, 136
discovering truth about

"Ernest," 41
on equal terms with men,
110–11
mistrusting Jack, 113
motive for marriage, 112
on name "Ernest," 39, 99,
115
perfection in, 173–74
preconceptions by, 129–30
trip to countryside, 46
insignificance of truth for,
156–58
inversion in, 133–34
Jack Worthing, 35–36
accepting Miss Prism as
his mother, 47, 103–104,
154
actors playing, 26, 36, 48,
54
appetite in, 176
asking for forgiveness,
128
christening of, 48–49
confronting "deceased"
brother, 128–29
contrasted with Miss
Prism's lack of emotion,
119–20
dandyism in, 145
deception by, 46
desire to escape, 93–94
discovering real origin,
41–42, 47, 94
dual selves of, 38–39, 92
exposed as a thief, 176–77
family background of, 94
on the female sex, 111
Lady Bracknell
disapproving of, 100
on marriage, 112
as moving back in time,
55–56
proposal to Gwendolen,
39, 116, 118

real identity revealed, 175
relationship with
Algernon, 91–92
scandals of, 47
search for a family by,
98–99
source of name for, 74–75
lack of father figures in, 99
lacking authenticity, 92–93
Lady Bracknell, 37–38
"English" claims by, 137
attitude toward the family,
153–54
on Bunbury's death, 117
on christening, 49
as conventional side of
Wilde's mother, 100, 101
dandyism in, 144–45, 149
disapproval of
engagement, 41
discovering real parentage
of Jack, 41–42
eating by, 95, 96
in first draft vs. final
version, 102
individualism in, 146
insensitivity of, 170
on Jack and Gwendolen's
engagement, 39–40
on Jack's origins, 96,
115–16, 117
on lower classes, 175
on marriage, 100–101, 113
and money, 49–50
preconceptions of, 130
on private property,
174–75
on requiring Jack to find a
family, 99
and social conventions,
117–19
source of name for, 75
and time, 131
turned into transvestite

role, 88
Lady Harbury, 123, 131
Lane (butler)
 on marriage, 163–64
 references to class
  through, 50
 source of name for, 75
Mary Farquhar, 101
Miss Prism, 37, 40
 as artistic side of Wilde's
  mother, 102–104
 dandyism in, 146
 disclosing secret of mix-
  up, 99
 emotional detachment of,
  119–20
 on female sex, 110, 111
 Jack accepting as his
  mother, 47, 103–104, 154
 mixing manuscript and
  baby, 41–42, 45, 46–47
 references to class
  through, 50
 source of name for, 75
 relationship to language in
  the play, 53–54
 "stock," 169
 Thomas Cardew, 47, 94
 as wearing social masks,
  122–23
 wish fulfillment vs. reality
  of, 128–30
Clarke, Sir Edward, 29
Cohen, Philip K., 125
Coppa, Francesca, 57
counterpoint, 165
"Critic as Artist, The," 71
Croft-Crooke, Rupert, 77

dandy/dandyism
 and aesthetics, 148–51
 and individualism, 142,
  146–47
 and middle-class morality,

 145–46
 as a philosophy/attitude
  toward life, 141–42
 self-centered focus on
  sensation in, 147–48
 as a subversive, 143–45
 through Dr. Chasuble,
  140–41
d'Aurevilly, Jules Barbey,
 142
"Decay of Lying, The," 71,
 116
"De Profundis," 31
determinism, 135–36
Disraeli, Benjamin, 142
Douglas, Lord Alfred, 28, 29,
 31–32, 87
Dramatic Review, 23
Duchess of Padua, The, 20

*Earnest, The Soul of Man
 Under Socialism,* 174
eating. *See* food/eating
Ellmann, Richard, 63, 100,
 173
Eltis, Sos, 105
Engaged (Gilbert), 73, 112,
 113
epigrams
 audience "in" on, 60–61
 Being Earnest as an, 61–62
 characteristics of, 58–59
 impersonal quality of,
  59–60
 and language of dandy, 85
 Wilde's use of, 57
 in Wilde's writing, 62–64
Error Corrected, The
 (Bunbury), 79

fairy tales
 Being Earnest as a, 126,
  130–31
 Wilde writing, 15, 23

food/eating
  characters engaged in, 49
  symbolizing unexpressed
    wishes, 95–96
  tediousness of, 168
Foundling, The (Lostocq), 62
Freud, Sigmund, 135

Ganz, Arthur, 140
gender roles, 159
  balance of, 110–11
  inversion of, 134–35
Gielgud, Sir John, 48
Gilbert, W.S., 45
  use of female characters,
    108, 109–10, 112
Great Expectations
  (Dickens), 52
Green, William, 74
Green Carnation, 66, 72
Guido Ferranti, 20
Guy Domville (James), 67

*Happy Prince and Other
  Tales, The*, 15, 23, 66, 126
Harding, Reginald, 76
Harris, Frank, 22, 33, 75
Heywood, John, 58
*History of Ancient
  Geography, A* (Bunbury),
  80
homosexuality
  connotations of, in
    Bunbury's name, 76–77
  of Oscar Wilde, 27–30, 134
  referenced in "Earnest"
    term, 89
  references to, in Wilde's
    writing, 72–73
  themes of, 86–88
  through intellectual
    seduction, 88–89
  Wilde confronting society
    on, 15–16

Horan, Patrick M., 97

Ideal Husband, An, 25,
  47–48, 66
  and *Being Earnest*
    as a parody on, 176–77
    based on, 172
    bond between male
      characters in, 84
    contrasted with *Being
      Earnest*, 70–71
    triviality in, 126
    the truth coming out in,
      128
*Importance of Being Earnest,
  The*
  compared with Gilbert's
    play, 109–10
  critical reviews of, 26–27,
    115
  deceit and deception in,
    92–93
  defying genre
    classification, 125–26
  detail in staging and
    performance of, 66–67
  as a fairy tale/fantasy, 126,
    130–31
  film version of, 54
  as genre of farce, 161–62
  influences on, 61–62
  lacking seriousness, 70
  omissions and deviations
    from other earlier plays,
    70–73
  opening performance of,
    26, 28–29, 65–66
  plot, 38–42, 52, 99
    dialogue sustaining,
      162–63
  private meaning in, 172–73
  revisions in, 67–68,
    105–106
  rooted in Wilde's earlier

plays, 172
survival of, 69–70
title, pun in, 87–89, 94–95,
115, 152, 153
as a verbal opera, 44–46
Wilde on, 127, 162
Wilde sending, to George
Alexander, 107
writing of, 25–26
see also characters;
language; parody; style;
themes
individualism, 146–47
Intentions, 66
inversion, 122–23, 133–35
Ives, George, 76

Jackson, Russell, 65
James, Henry, 59, 61, 67

Kiberd, Declan, 132
Kohl, Norbert, 114

Labiche, Eugene, 45
Lady Windermere's Fan , 24,
66
bond between male
characters in, 84
contrasted with *Being
Earnest,* 70–71
mother character in, 98,
101–102
Victorian morality in, 52
Lane, John, 75
Langtry, Lily, 15
language
of dandy, 84–86
dialogue, sustaining plot,
162–63
as evading analysis, 83–84
as more important than
characters, 35
and pleasure, 54–55
and prattle, 55–56

pun on "Earnest"/"Ernest,"
87–89, 94–95, 115, 152,
153
relationship to characters,
93
self-sufficiency of, 53
Laws (Plato), 54
"Le Dandy" (Baudelaire),
142
Lestocq, W., 62
Leverson, Ada, 72, 76
*Lippincott's Monthly
Magazine,* 23–24
Lloyd, Constance (wife),
21–23, 31, 32
Lockridge, Norman, 58
"Lord Arthur Savile's
Crime," 172, 173–74

Mahaffy, Reverend J.P., 18,
23, 81
marriage
Lady Bracknell on an ideal,
100–102, 113
satire on Victorian
approach to, 117, 118–19
theme of, 48
Wilde's revisions changing
portrayal of, 111–13
Marx, Karl, 133, 135
Mason, A.E.W., 66
Maturin, Charles Robert, 31
Maurier, George du, 24
McCarthy, Mary, 167
criticism on *Being Earnest,*
54–55
polar responses to *Being
Earnest,* 86
on pun in title, 87–88
Melmoth, Sebastion, 31
*Midsummer's Night Dream,
A* (Shakespeare), 126
Miles, Frank, 19
money, importance of, 49–50

Monty Python, 52

names
  Jack "Worthing," 94
  sources of "Bunbury,"
    75–82
  in Wilde's writing, 74–75
Nassaar, Christopher S., 171
New York Times
  (newspaper), 32
Nietzsche, Friedrich, 165
No Exit (Sartre), 55–56

"Oscar Polka Mazurka," 33
O'Sullivan, Vincent, 81
Oxford University, 18

Palace of Truth, The
  (Gilbert), 108
Pall Mall Gazette, 23
paradox, 85, 122–23
Parker, David, 152
parody
  on *An Ideal Husband,*
    176–77
  on "Lord Arthur Savile's
    Crime," 173–74
  on *The Picture of Dorian
    Gray,* 175
  on *Salome,* 176
Pater, Walter, 18, 115, 147
Patience, 19
"Personal Impressions of
  America," 21
Picture of Dorian Gray, The,
  23–24, 66, 71
  and *Being Earnest*
    as a parody on, 175
    based on, 172
    mother character in, 98,
      102
Plato, 54
Portora Royal School, 17
"Portrait of Mr. W.H.," 71–72

Powell, Kerry, 61–62
proverbs, 58–59
pun
  on "Earnest"/"Ernest,"
    87–89, 94–95, 152, 153
Punch (magazine), 24, 72

Queensberry, Lord, 28–29,
  87, 168

Rank, Otto, 137, 138
"Ravenna," 18–19
Reading Gaol prison, 30
realism, 127
Redgrave, Michael, 54
Robins, Elizabeth, 61
Rosenfeld, M.H., 33
Ross, Robert, 27, 31, 32, 69
Rothenstein, Sir William, 81
Ruskin, John, 18

Salome, 24–25, 129, 172
  and *Being Earnest*
    as a parody on, 176
    based on, 172
Sartre, Jean-Paul, 55–56
Shakespeare, William, 48,
  126
Shaw, George Bernard, 77
  contrasted with Wilde, 162
  criticism by, 25, 54–55, 168
  on laughter from the play,
    85, 86
Shelley, Percy Bysshe, 133
"Soul of Man Under
  Socialism, The" (Wilde), 23
Sperenza. *See* Wilde, Lady
  Jane Francesca Elgee
Stahl, W.H., 80
Stern, Erich, 137
*Studies in the History of the
  Renaissance* (Pater), 18
style
  for comic effect, 116–17

as formula for humor, 169–70
paradox, use of, 122–23
topic skimming, 162–65
use of
counterpoint, 165
inversion, 133–35
Sullivan, Arthur, 45
Sweethearts (Gilbert), 109
symbolism
Bunbury, 137
country/city, 93
food, 95–96
Symons, Arthur, 141

themes
Anglo-Irish relations, 136–37
conventional notions of family broken down, 153–54
dandyism, 143–52
defining human identity, 152–54
dissolution of human identity, 154–56
homosexuality, 86–88
hypocrisy
of high society, 96
of Victorian style and etiquette, 115–16
insignificance of truth, 156–57
lack of seriousness, 171–72
love as impulse, 156
nothingness, 154
pain and pleasure, 54–55
rejection of determinism, 135–36
reversal of gender roles, 134–35
self-parody in earlier works, 172–77
skimming over of, 162–65

triviality, 126–28
Victorian solemnity, 162
Thomazine, Emily, 100
Trinity College, 18
"Trivial Comedy for Serious People," 67
Turner, Reginald, 55
Tyrrell, Robert Yelverton, 18

Ulrichs, Karl Heinrich, 89
United States
Wilde lecturing in, 19–20

Vera, 20

Walkley, A.B., 77
Ward, William, 76
Wells, H.G., 77
Whistler, James McNeill, 21
Wilde, Colonel de, 16
Wilde, Constance Lloyd (wife), 21–23, 31, 32
Wilde, Cyril (son), 22
Wilde, Isole Francesca (sister), 17
Wilde, Lady Jane Francesca Elgee (mother), 16–17, 30
Lady Bracknell character as conventional side of, 100–101
Miss Prism as artistic side of, 102–104
presence in Wilde's comedies, 98, 101–102
Wilde, Oscar
on abolition of private property, 174
accomplishments, 15
after prison, 31–32
in America, 19–20
arrest/trial of, 27, 29–30
attire, 19
on Bohemianism, 165
childhood, 16–17

college years, 18–19
death of, 32–33
homosexuality of, 15–16,
    27–29, 134
on *The Importance of Being
    Earnest*, 70, 127, 162
as an individualist, 146–47
lecturing in England, 21
link with Sir Edward
    Bunbury, 81–82
marriage, 21–23
on pain and pleasure, 55
in prison, 30–31
public personality, 24
on role as writer, 63
on sincerity, 133
taste for publicity, 68–69
on triviality, 116, 126–27
unhappy ending in life of,
    15, 16
writing by, 66
  basing plays on earlier
    plays, 172
  Being Earnest vs. earlier
    plays, 70–73
  comic opera, 19
  critique of antithesis in,
    132–33
  dandyism in, 84, 141–44
  fairy tales, 15, 23
  as imposing opinions on
    audience, 167–68
  influences, 61–62

journalism, 23
  mother characters in, 98,
    101–102
  novels, 23–24
  plays, 20, 24–25
  poetry, 18–19, 20, 31
  use of epigrams, 57–60,
    60, 62–64
  use of names, 74–75
Wilde, Thomas
    (grandfather), 16
Wilde, Vyvyan (son), 22
Wilde, William (father), 16
Wilde, William Wills
    (brother), 17–19
Woman of No Importance, A,
    25, 47, 53, 66
  Being Earnest based on,
    172
  bond between male
    characters in, 84
  contrasted with *Being
    Earnest*, 70–71
  mother character in, 98
  the truth coming out in,
    128
Woman's World (magazine),
    23
Women's Liberal
    Association, 22
World's Wit and Wisdom
    (Lockridge), 58
Wyndham, Charles, 67